# BACKPACKER'S GUIDE

# BACKPACKER'S GUIDE

by W. R. C. Shedenhelm

WORLD

World Publications, Inc.
Mountain View, California

**Library of Congress Cataloging in Publication Data**

Shedenhelm, W R C, 1924-
  The backpacker's guide.

  1. Backpacking. I. Title.
GV199.6.S536      796.5      78-27875
ISBN 0-89037-210-1

© 1979 by
W R C Shedenhelm

World Publications, Inc.
Mountain View, CA

To Richard Scott Shedenhelm and a whole new generation of backpackers and mountain walkers.

# Contents

# Prologue

*How can you buy or sell the sky, the warmth of the land? The idea is strange to us.*

*If we do not own the freshness of the air and the sparkle of the water, how can you buy them?*

*Every part of this earth is sacred to my people. Every shining pine needle, every sandy shore, every mist in the dark woods, every clearing and humming insect is holy in the memory and experience of my people. The sap which courses through the trees carries the memories of the red man.*

*The white man's dead forget the country of their birth when they go to walk among the stars. Our dead never forget this beautiful earth, for it is the mother of the red man. We are a part of the earth and it is part of us. The perfumed flowers are our sisters; the deer, the horse, the great eagle, these are our brothers. The rocky crests, the juices in the meadows, the body heat of the pony, and man—all belong to the same family.*

*So, when the Great Chief in Washington sends word that he wishes to buy our land, he asks much of us. The Great Chief sends word he will reserve us a place so that we can live comfortably to ourselves. He will be our father and we will be his children. So we will consider your offer to buy our land. But it will not be easy. For this land is sacred to us.*

*This shining water that moves in the streams and rivers is not*

1

*just water but the blood of our ancestors. If we sell you the land, you must remember that it is sacred, and you must teach your children that it is sacred and that each ghostly reflection in the clear water of the lakes tells of events and memories in the life of my people. The water's murmur is the voice of my father's father.*

*The rivers are our brothers, they quench our thirsts. The rivers carry our canoes, they feed our children. If we sell you our land, you must remember, and teach your children, that the rivers are our brothers, and yours, and you must henceforth give the rivers the kindness you would give any brother.*

*We know that the white man does not understand our ways. One portion of the land is the same to him as the next, for he is a stranger who comes in the night and takes from the land what he needs. The earth is not his brother, but his enemy, and when he has conquered it, he moves on. He leaves his father's grave behind, and he does not care. His father's graves and his children's birthright are forgotten. He treats his mother, the earth, and his brother, the sky, as things to be bought, plundered, sold like sheep or bright beads. His appetite will devour the earth and leave behind only a desert.*

*I do not know. Our ways are different from your ways. The sight of your cities pains the eyes of the red man. But perhaps it is because the red man is a savage and does not understand.*

*There is not quiet place in the white man's cities. No place to hear the unfurling of leaves in the spring, or the rustle of an insect's wings. But perhaps it is because I am a savage and do not understand. The clatter only seems to insult the ears. And what is there to life if a man cannot hear the lonely cry of the whippoorwill or the arguments of the frogs around a pond at night? I am a red man and do not understand. The Indian prefers the soft sound of the wind darting over the face of a pond, the smell of the wind itself, cleansed by a mid-day rain, or scented with the pinon pine.*

*The air is precious to the red man, for all things share the same breath—the beast, the tree, the man, they all share the same breath. The white man does not seem to notice the air he breathes. Like a man dying for many days, he is numb to the stench. But if we sell you our land, you must remember that the air is precious to us, that the air shares its spirit with all the life it supports. The wind that gave our grandfather his first breath also received his last sigh. And if we sell you our land, you must keep it apart and sacred, as a place where even white man can go to taste the wind that is sweetened by the meadow's flowers.*

*So we will consider your offer to buy our land. If we decide to accept, I will make one condition: The white man must treat the beasts of this land like his brothers.*

*I am a savage and do not understand any other way. I have seen a thousand rotting buffalos on the prairie, left by the white man who shot them from a passing train. I am a savage and do not understand how the smoking iron horse can be more important than the buffalo that we kill only to stay alive.*

*What is man without the beasts? If all the beasts were gone, man would die from a great loneliness of spirit. For whatever happens to the beasts, soon happens to man. All things are connected.*

*You must teach your children that the ground beneath their feet is the ashes of our grandfathers. So that they will respect the land, tell your children that the earth is rich with the lives of our kin. Teach your children what we have taught our children, that the earth is our mother. Whatever befalls the earth befalls the sons of the earth. If men spit upon the ground, they spit upon themselves.*

*This we know: The earth does not belong to man; man belongs to the earth. This we know. All things are connected like the blood which unites one family. All things are connected.*

*Whatever befalls the earth befalls the sons of the earth. Man did not weave the web of life; he is merely a strand in it. Whatever he does to the web, he does to himself.*

*Even the white man, whose God walks and talks with him as friend to friend, cannot be exempt from the common destiny. We may be brothers after all. We shall see. One thing we know, which the white man may one day discover—our God is the same God. You may think now that you own Him as you wish to own our land; but you cannot. He is the God of man, and His compassion is equal for the red man and the white. This earth is precious to Him, and to harm the earth is to heap contempt on its creator. The whites too shall pass; perhaps sooner than all the other tribes. Contaminate your bed, and you will one night suffocate in your own waste.*

*But in your perishing you will shine brightly, fired by the strength of the God who brought you to this land and for some special purpose gave you dominion over this land and over the red man. That destiny is a mystery to us, for we do not understand when the buffalo are all slaughtered, the wild horses are tamed, the secret corners of the forest heavy with the scent of many men, the view of the ripe hills blotted with talking wires. Where is the thicket? Gone. Where is the eagle? Gone. The end of living and the beginning of survival.*

**Chief Seattle
Duwamish Tribe
1854**

# Introduction

The fascination with backpacking over any other form of travel is really quite simple. When backpacking, you are completely self-contained. You are carrying your home on your back. You can walk as far as you like within the limits of physical endurance and your food supply. You can stop anywhere you wish, to spend the night or to spend a week. You have thrown off a great deal of the material world and are back to basics. You are, for a short time at least, totally self-sufficient.

In recent years we have been relearning that the natural world around us—the mountains, deserts, and seas—is a fragile and critical part of our existence on this planet Earth. Backpackers, being closer to the primitive earth than most other people, have long been aware of this. But even within this group, the awareness has grown within the last few years. Although there has been an explosive increase in the number of backpackers in our wilderness, I truly believe that I find less littering and less vandalism than I did a decade or two ago. And this is good.

The expression *minimum impact* is tossed around a lot now in writing about the outdoors, and it is an important concept. If we are to keep the land beautiful for ourselves and for future generations, it is essential to use the land and to leave it as nearly untouched as when we first saw it. This light tread on the land consists of many little habits and practices that we must recognize and adopt. That is part of what this book is about.

Some of this awareness consists in watching out for business interests which would be happy to destroy our wildernesses "because industry and the country need the timber and the minerals." That may be, but I think my country needs the wilderness even more. At a later date any part of the wilderness can be mined or logged, but in the other direction the process is irreversible. The Rubaiyat of Omar Khayyam says: "The

*Grand Teton National Park, Wyoming (Wyoming Travel Commission)*

moving finger writes; and, having writ, moves on: nor all your piety nor wit shall lure it back to cancel half a line, nor all your tears wash out a word of it."

That is how I feel about allowing any further destruction of our remaining wilderness.

It is up to us, then, you and me, to keep our mountains and deserts as new and shining as they were the first day that man saw them. We must try to become a part of the land, leaving no signs that we have been there, trampling on it. This attitude need not be some all-consuming backpacker's quest, like a Don Quixote on foot, but is largely a matter of cleaning up after ourselves and others. It is a matter of caring, of accepting the principle that we can't and shouldn't try to conquer nature, but should become a living part of it.

Backpacking is a way of seeing things, a way of life, or, at least, an approach to life. It is feeling the earth revolve, as against only believing that it revolves. It is seeing the annual renewal of life, and the slower renewal of the land. It is sensing your place amongst the rabbits, and the frogs, and the eagles. And it is understanding that nature is neither good nor bad, kind nor vicious, but that it simply is.

Walt Kelly's Pogo once paraphrased Admiral Perry's "We have met the enemy, and he is ours," to read, "We have met the enemy, and he is us." What I have discovered in backpacking is that Pogo is correct only in part. What he should have said was, "We have met the enemy of the earth, and he is us. We have also met the friend of the earth, and he is us, too."

# 1

# Learning to Walk

If you are not yet an experienced backpacker, and have ever stood at a trailhead watching gung-ho experienced backpackers come down the trail, back from the hills, you may have been somewhat deceived. The backpackers stride into the roadhead parking lot, their huge packs seemingly weightless, their skins glossy and tanned. Lord! To be so ruddy healthy!

Well, you're right overall, but there are a few factors you may have overlooked. First, their packs *are* weightless relative to what they weighed a week or so ago because each backpacker has consumed several pounds of food and used most of their stove fuel. Second, their beautiful tans are not due to sunshine and healthful living, although they have had plenty of these. The sleek glossiness is mostly due to many layers of Sea & Ski sun cream, plus an equally-large number of layers of Cutter's insect repellent. The tan itself is a combination of trail dust and campfire soot.

Let it be understood that very few backpackers consider cleanliness to be directly related to godliness. I don't mean to imply that backpackers are unclean. It's just that backpackers believe over-bathing to be a waste of time while in the wilderness. As long as the coloration is even, leave it alone.

Once the backpacker returns to the mundane, civilized world, a thorough shower and a change of clothes should be taken care of as soon as practical. One of the tragedies of backpacking is watching your glowing tan disappear through a hole in the shower floor.

Backpackers, on the whole, are healthy and in good physical condition. They simply wouldn't be there, couldn't be there, if they were not in good shape. I do have my doubts, however, about whether the act of backpacking makes the participants that way. There's a similar argument of cause and effect in running. One opinion is that running obviously makes a person healthy; just look at the runners. The contrasting opinion is that only people who are basically healthy take up running in the first place.

Both of these opinions are very likely partially true, and the same reasoning can be used for backpackers. If you are interested enough in backpacking to be reading this book, it is likely that you are already in good enough physical condition to go backpacking.

The beauty of backpacking, as I mentioned earlier, is that you carry your complete outdoor home on your back and become a physically independent entity. This means that you can stop anytime or anywhere you desire. You don't have to walk ten miles a day; not even five. You can start by backpacking 200 yards if you wish. You can camp at a remote

*Grand Teton National Park,    Wyoming   (Wyoming Travel Commission)*

*Santa Monica Mountains, California*

lake for a week, or you can cross a mountain range. You can backpack in California or in Nepal. You can go out with a dozen people, or you can wander the hills alone. Once you have learned your craft, you are self-sufficient and physically free to travel almost anywhere you want to go.

Now, I assume that you already know how to walk. Backpacking, however, requires a different kind of walking than usual because you are hiking up and down hills, on trails and cross-country, for long periods of time each day, with from 30 to 50 pounds in your backpack.

You should also add to these differences in walking "The Law of Backpacking" which I derived through many lonely hours on the trail, tongue in cheek:

Any trail, whether it begins and ends at the same point and elevation, will have more uphill sections than level or downhill sections, regardless of the direction of travel.

As any experienced backpacker knows, this "phenomenon of uphilledness" will increase in intensity based on the weight of one's backpack, and the lateness in the day. One explanation is based on the process in tectonic geology known as "isostacy." This would claim that the weight of the backpacker and his pack press downwards on the surface of the earth, making a dent. The backpacker is then, in effect and in actuality, constantly walking up out of a hole. This would be much more noticeable late on a summer's day, when the heat of the sun has softened the earth's crust considerably. From my studies as a graduate geologist, I find that some experts consider the earth to be very much like a giant ball of taffy, while others think of it as more like a Gouda cheese. Obviously more geophysical research is needed.

Kenneth Cooper, M.D., in his books *Aerobics,* and *New Aerobics,* lists the relative exercise values of many sports and activities, but does not include backpacking. For my personal records, I used to value miles backpacked as equivalent to miles jogged or run. I valued day hikes, with a light pack, at one-half jogging's value. The reasons for this is that in backpacking you're usually doing your walking at high elevations, where the amount of available oxygen is less, plus you're carrying an extra quarter or so of your body-weight on your back. This is why you need to learn to walk smoothly and with economy in the mountains.

Epictetus, the Roman philosopher who lived at the time of Nero and Hadrian, wrote in his "Discourses:"

> Every habit and faculty is maintained and increased by the corresponding actions: the habit of walking by walking, the habit of running by running. If you would be a good reader, read; if a writer, write. But when you shall not read for thirty days in succession, but have done something else, you will know the consequence. In the same way, if you shall have lain down for ten days, get up and attempt to make a long

walk, and you will see how your legs are weakened. Generally, then, if you would make anything a habit, do it; if you would not make it a habit, do not do it, but accustom yourself to do something else in place of it.

Epictetus' statement, written about 100 AD, may seem a little obvious, but actually it isn't. If you want to be a good mountain walker, you have to walk in the mountains. Jogging and running will help, of course, but they are not a replacement for the high country. In the backpacking off-seasons I try to run a couple of miles every other day. I do this mainly to stay in reasonably good physical condition. It is a means, though, rather than an end in itself. The end product is to enjoy backpacking. The stronger leg muscles and more efficient cardio-vascular system that running develops makes the early-season backpacking easier, safer, and more pleasant. But there should always be a break-in period on that first backpacking trip after several month's layoff, to get used to the weight of the backpack and to the uneven ground.

If you have never been backpacking or not for a long time, there is an easy way to build up to it and pace yourself, earning special awards as you progress. This is the Presidential Sports Award program run by the President's Council on Physical Fitness and Sports. The program currently covers 43 sports, from Archery to Weight Lifting. Completion is based on the participant spending 50 hours, spread over 50 activity periods where possible, within a four month time span in any of the sports listed. Upon completion of each program, the participant will receive a certificate signed by the President of the United States, and an embroidered patch which can be sewn to a jacket or a pack.

The sports within this program which would be of special interest to us, if we are building up to backpacking and mountain walking from the beginning would be Fitness Walking, Jogging, possibly Running, and Back Packing. The Council spells it as two words; why I cannot say. Other awardable sports which could conceivably be of use to us in physical conditioning include Bicycling and Swimming. Extensions beyond backpacking could include Climbing, Orienteering, and Skiing (Nordic). The Fitness Walking award required 125 miles of walking, at

*Santa Monica Mountains, California*

a minimum speed of four miles an hour, each session without pause or rest, and with no more than 2½ miles per day to be counted. Four miles an hour is a brisk walk; the standard U.S. Army marching pace is three miles an hour.

The Jogging award is essentially the same as for Fitness Walking: 125 miles, with no more than 2½ miles credited per day. As mentioned, the totals must be achieved within a four-month period.

Running requires a minimum of 200 miles, with a daily minimum of three and a maximum of five miles. You must make each run without a stop, so as to average better than nine minutes per mile.

The Back Packing award avoids the wide variances of speeds over different terrain by basing its requirements on time or duration. For this award you must backpack a minimum of 50 hours within the four-month period, with no more than three hours in any one day credited to the total. And your pack must weigh at least ten percent of your body weight. This last is obviously to eliminate day hikes with a light pack.

Divide 50 hours by the three allowed per day, and you end up with 16.66 days, if you get in a full three hours each day. It's not fair to move the extra hours from a six or eight hour day into a shorter day. I've earned the Back Packing Award the last four summers (two Fords, and two Carters), and I've had to do some last-minute scrambling to fill in for all those 1½ and 2½ hours days on the trail. With longer daily averages, you could receive the award in 17 days.

I find it much easier to get things done if I have a plan, an objective. It is always much easier not to do things which require strenuous physical or mental work. This is why, when I started jogging a few years ago, I worked towards the various progressive awards of the National Jogging Association. During that first year I earned ribbons and patches for jogging 76 miles, then 200 miles, 365 kilometers, 365 miles, and finally 1000 kilometers. I wasn't jogging so that I could get the awards, but getting them did give me a series of objectives that I could actually see ahead of me. You may not need this sort of carrot-before-the-donkey prize system, but it helped me a great deal. It is two different things to know that something is beneficial—physically, mentally, or morally—and to actually do something about it. It is so much easier and less complicated to sit in a bar, rather than to run three miles in the park. While I'll admit that awards such as these are childish and absurd, they are part of my slender arsenal of weapons in the constant battle against sloth.

Then, start some weekend day hikes with a light pack. The amount of physical energy consumed in mountain walking is really impressive. Everytime you gain a foot of elevation, you are lifting the total weight of your body and your pack that much. Let's say that you gross out at 150 pounds, and you gain 500 feet (a quite moderate gain) on a hike. That's 75,000 foot-pounds of work. If you were to lift a 50 pound barbell from the floor to over your head, a vertical distance of eight feet, you would have to do so 188 times to equal the work that you did quite easily on your hike. The mere thought of doing 188 full presses with a 50 pound barbell makes my eyes glaze over.

But don't forget that to get your body used to mountain walking, you must do mountain walking. Jogging and running will help, most assuredly, but the final conditioning will only come from spending time on the mountain trails.

There are only a few things that I can tell you about how best to walk in the mountains. Most of it you will pick up by trial-and-error, by slowly adapting your style of walking to the special conditions of mountain walking. Very few mountain trails are smooth, for example, so you can't shuffle along without raising your feet at all, as you may do on sidewalks. But the idea still is not to raise your feet any more than is necessary on the trail, wasting energy for naught. Try to walk as smoothly and as effortlessly as possible. Don't walk in short stop-and-go sprints. This is not only inefficient, but will also drive the hiker behind you out of his mind. Try to flow as much as you can. Keep a slow, steady pace uphill, stretch out your stride on the level sections, back off again downhill.

Take time to look at the scenery; that's why you're in the mountains. Don't walk so close to the person ahead of you that all you see is the back of his pack. You always want to be able to see the trail 20 to 100 feet ahead, to subconsciously prepare for the irregularities that the trail is certain to have. Don't step over rocks and logs, if you can step around them. Don't cut switchbacks on the trail. It not only leads to more rapid erosion of the hillside, but it breaks the slow rhythm of your stride.

When you decide it's time for a rest stop and you smoke, it only makes sense that you should not do so while walking through the woods, or anywhere else. Stop and sit down in a clear area where there is nothing on the ground that could conceivably catch on fire. After you have lit your pipe or coffin nail, blow out the match, wait a few seconds, then squeeze the burnt tip with your fingers to make certain that it is cool. Now drop the burnt match into your shirt pocket, along with the filters off your cigarettes, for disposal later. Now wasn't that neat? Smokey the Bear would be proud of you!

*Selway-Bitterroot area, Idaho  (Idaho Division of Tourism and Industrial Development)*

One of the many advantages of hiking and backpacking alone is that you can stop for a rest whenever you feel like it. If you are leading a group, there is a tendency to stride on, showing off your physical superiority. If you are not the leader, you will often curse whoever is for not stopping often nor long enough.

When backpacking alone, I sometimes get so swept away

with the ease and joy of walking a particular section of trail that I go on an hour or two without a stop. At other times, on long uphill sections, I may stop every few feet for five or ten seconds of deep breathing. Many authorities claim that you should never get so out-of-breath backpacking that you could not hold a conversation with someone while walking.

The advantage of the physical conditioning that we have mentioned and highly recommend, is that you start far ahead of the unprepared slobs who aren't in shape. You'll still have to make physical adjustments to the thinness of the mountain air and the weight of the backpack, but other than these, you'll be a Sherpa Tiger!

You may find that a particular leader, whom you cursed last year for not making enough rest stops, this year is making far too many.

But it's not him. It's you.

# 2

# Planning is Everything

While every backpacking trip should be an adventure of sorts, only careful planning can keep it from being a misadventure. Careful planning, by its very nature, would seem to suppress much of the feeling of freedom that makes backpacking so enjoyable. Perhaps. But if this careful planning is taken care of before you start on the actual backpack trip, then you can be truly free from worries while on that trip. And that's the whole idea!

By smugly thinking that I was superior to having to use a backpacking equipment check list, I have ended up far into the mountains without nylon cord for rigging a shelter one time, long pants for the cold evenings another, and even a pot to cook in one time. And I was certain that I had put everything essential into the backpack—from memory.

I'll give you my basic list, which has evolved over the years. Feel free to add items in the blank spaces or to cross out any you feel you don't need. The essentials will vary with the time of year, the type of terrain, the possible weather, and whether you're going alone or in a group. But *always* go over the check list as you pack, even though you are not planning to take everything on the list. At least you will know what you are not taking.

I have found, too, that trying to pack the morning of a trip frequently leads to disaster. Pack at least two days before the start. Then unload everything, reconsider the importance of each piece, and try to repack more efficiently.

If you must pack at the last minute, a checklist is critically necessary. Once, after hastily packing with a hangover, I arrived at a distant roadhead to find that I had failed to bring my boots!

This list includes some items with duplicate functions. You will normally only carry one version of whatever it is. Having both on the list will help make sure that you take at least one. We'll talk about the differences and their values later.

- ☐ Map of the area
- ☐ Compass
- ☐ Flashlight
- ☐ Sunglasses
- ☐ Extra food and water
- ☐ Extra clothing
- ☐ Waterproof matches
- ☐ Candle or fuel tablets
- ☐ Pocket knife
- ☐ First-aid kit
- ☐ Sleeping bag
- ☐ Ensolite pad
- ☐ Air mattress
- ☐ Air mattress repair kit
- ☐ Pillow
- ☐ Ground cloth
- ☐ Tent
- ☐ Tarp
- ☐ Nylon cord
- ☐ Tent pegs
- ☐ Backpack
- ☐ Summit pack
- ☐ Stove
- ☐ Fuel can, full
- ☐ Matches
- ☐ Grill
- ☐ Cooking pot, lid
- ☐ Plastic bowl
- ☐ Sierra or plastic cup
- ☐ Spoon
- ☐ Water bottles, 1-liter
- ☐ Camp water carrier
- ☐ Extra flashlight batteries, bulb
- ☐ Toilet paper
- ☐ Soap and towel
- ☐ Boots
- ☐ Wind parka
- ☐ Long-sleeved shirt
- ☐ Sweater
- ☐ Short pants
- ☐ Long pants
- ☐ Belt
- ☐ Rain parka
- ☐ Rain pants
- ☐ Cotton socks
- ☐ Wool socks
- ☐ Camp shoes
- ☐ Extra underwear
- ☐ Bandanas
- ☐ Wool gloves
- ☐ Wool mittens
- ☐ Toilet kit

- ☐ Clothespins
- ☐ Snow goggles
- ☐ Suntan lotion
- ☐ Insect repellent
- ☐ Small notebook
- ☐ Ballpoint pen
- ☐ Regional guidebook
- ☐ Binoculars
- ☐ Camera
- ☐ _____
- ☐ _____

- ☐ Tripod
- ☐ Tripod-head clamp
- ☐ Crampons
- ☐ Ice axe
- ☐ Steel-tipped cane
- ☐ Sun hat
- ☐ Balaclava
- ☐ Climbing rope
- ☐ _____
- ☐ _____
- ☐ _____

Every time you get ready to load up your pack, run down this list to make certain that you haven't forgotten anything. If you do leave some items behind, make it by choice and not by accident.

After each trip, when you unpack, notice which items you did not use, and plan not to take them again unless they were carried basically for emergencies. For example, you would never leave the Ten Essentials behind if you had any sense whatsoever, not even when you only plan a quick dash up a nearby peak.

Just as a child in an unfamiliar place is happier with a toy from home, many adult backpackers will tolerate a little extra weight to carry some personal item which is not truly essential.

One girl I knew tied a small, stuffed teddy bear to her pack during the day and to her tent at night. Another backpacker always carried a delicate sparkling martini glass for his evening cocktails. Another a hardbound copy of Thoreau's *Walden.* My failing is a silver-mounted Finnish sheath knife, set with green cabochons of self-mined chrysocolla, the whole based somewhat fancifully on my reading of Tolkien's *Lord of the Rings* trilogy.

The early planning of any trip should include a thorough reading of the guide books available for the region, and many hours spent mooning over Geological Survey and Park or Forest Services maps. I receive as much enjoyment and information from my study of the maps as I would from several guidebooks.

By the time I start on my backpack trip, I have gone over the topography so many times on the maps that it would be almost impossible for me to really get lost. I may not know the country like the back of my hand in advance, but I certainly know it like the back of my head.

The United States Geological Survey topographic maps are the finest landform maps for this country, and each contains a wealth of information. They can get quite out-of-date insofar as manmade features go: roads, buildings, dams, trails. But the surface of the land is unchanging during the lifetimes of you, me, and the USGS. With contour lines showing equal elevations above sea level, you can plan for the gradients that you will encounter on various portions of your trip. You can update the roads and trails from the more current Forest Service or Park Service maps, which are fine for this sort of information, but almost never tell you anything about trail gradients or other than the elevations of peaks and occasional passes.

For U.S. Geological Survey topographical maps of areas east of the Mississippi River, including Minnesota, Puerto Rico, and the Virgin Islands, write to: Branch of Distribution, U.S. Geological Survey, 1200 S. Eads Street, Arlington, Virginia 22202.

For areas west of the Mississippi, including Alaska, Hawaii, Louisiana, Guam, and American Samoa, write: Branch of Distribution, U.S. Geological Survey, Box 25286, Federal Center, Denver, Colorado 80225.

Residents of Alaska may order Alaska maps from: Distribution Section, U.S. Geological Survey, Federal Building, Box 12, 101 Twelfth Street, Fairbanks, Alaska 99701.

Topographical maps are available over the counter at the following U.S. Geological Survey offices, all of which are authorized agents of the Superintendent of Documents.

Anchorage, Alaska—Skyline Building, 508 Second Avenue, Room 108.
Fairbanks, Alaska—Federal Building, 101 Twelfth Avenue.
Los Angeles, California—Federal Building, 300 N. Los Angeles Street, Room 7638.
Menlo Park, California—345 Middlefield Road.

*Mt. Whitney Trail, Inyo National Forest*

San Francisco, California—Customhouse, 555 Battery Street, Room 504.

Denver, Colorado—Federal Building, 1961 Stout Street, Room 169.

Denver, Colorado—Federal Center, Building 41.

Rolla, Missouri—1400 Independence Road.

Dallas, Texas—Federal Building, 1100 Commerce Street, Room 1C45.

Salt Lake City, Utah—Federal Building, 125 S. State Street, Room 8105.

Reston, Virginia—302 National Center, 12201 Sunrise Valley Drive, Room 1C402.

Spokane, Washington—U.S. Courthouse, West 920 Riverside Avenue, Room 678.

Washington, D.C.—General Services Building, 19th & F Streets, N.W., Room 1028.

U.S. Geological Survey maps are also sold by some 1650 commercial dealers throughout the United States. Dealers are listed in the State Indexes to Topographical Maps, which are obtained free of charge by mail or over the counter from the offices listed above.

Many of the most interesting parts of this country for backpacking are national wilderness areas. These supersede and outrank the national forests and national parks which they often overlap. Although there are some variations, you can expect that in a designated wilderness area no motorized vehicles or other equipment will be allowed, that there will be no private dwellings, roads, power lines, developed public campgrounds or other developed recreational facilities. Mining and grazing are severely restricted. The construction of rock walls, large fireplaces or fire rings, shelters, bough beds, bridges, dams, latrines, and other things that will alter the natural character of the land are not permitted.

Unless you are doing a scientific study and have written permission from the appropriate forest or park supervisor, you may not collect plants, animals, minerals, or historical items within a wilderness area. The national park sections within (or without) a wilderness area also prohibit pets (on or off leashes), firearms (loaded or unloaded), hunting, shooting, molesting, or disturbing any wildlife. Fishing is allowed in every wilderness area that I know of, but only under the fishing regulations of the state in which the wilderness area lies. Hunting within the national forest sections of the wilderness areas is similarly under the regulation of the state in which it lies.

To hike or backpack in these wilderness areas, alone or as a group, you must secure a wilderness permit from the head-quarters of the national forest or the national park through which you enter the wilderness—not the one in which most of your trip will be, but that containing your point of entry. Attached to the permit will be a list of any special regulations or limitations that apply to the specific areas of your travel.

Now, you can apply for your wilderness permit when you arrive at your starting point, but it is much safer to write for it months in advance. Heavily-used areas often have daily quotas, and half or more of the permits for any given day are given out in advance. In the wilderness areas I know, you can send for your permits for the coming summer by February 1. If you wait until the last minute, you might find the quota filled for several days, particularly around a major holiday weekend.

It is necessary that I plan my backpacking trip dates quite precisely, based around my magazine's (*Rock & Gem*) editorial schedule. Having my coming summer and autumn wilderness permits all safely signed, sealed, and delivered therefore makes one less thing to worry about. If you send for a permit and then cannot make the particular trip, mail the permit back or tele-phone the ranger station that issued it. This way someone else can use your space in the day's quota, if there is one in use.

With my permits secured, I know that I can always cancel out, while it could prove difficult to cancel in.

On most state and federal land, you will need a fire permit to build a campfire anywhere outside of a posted public camp-ground or picnic area. Check with the ranger station in the area. Your wilderness permit, though, is also a fire permit.

Only one wilderness permit is necessary for a group travelling together. It would be a good idea to give each person in the backpacking group a photocopy of the permit, in case the group should split up for any reason.

If it is at all possible, and it usually is, I plan my backpacks so that I can spend the night of the final day in a motel near the trailhead. After a week or more on the trail, a hot shower, clean clothes, and a soft bed are pure heaven. A 300-mile drive home in the afternoon sun is not. I always leave an overnight bag in the van with a complete change of clothes, comfortable shoes, razor and shampoo. I make a motel reservation before the trip or on the way to the roadhead. Then I have all bases covered.

If you wish to lead others on an organized trip, your planning must be even more thorough, as you are responsible for their safety, for selecting comfortable and interesting campsites, and for keeping the daily travel well within their capabilities. Even though you specify certain minimum requirements and experience in advance, you are bound to get someone from time to time, who cannot walk the distances happily, who wants to go farther, who doesn't have all the proper equipment, who lags far behind the group, or talks too much. These are just a few of the crosses you will have to bear if you want to be a big cheese trip leader. Some people enjoy this sort of thing immensely; others prefer to do their backpacking solo or only with a close friend or relative. This is something that you must decide for yourself, by trial and error. As in many other fields, there is no substitute for experience.

If you are going to be a backpack trip leader, you most certainly should set a limit on the size of your group in advance. The national parks currently limit backpacking and other overnight groups to 25 people. Fifteen is recommended, and is enforced in some high-density or particularly-fragile areas. In one of its publications the forest service recommends, but does not enforce, groups of eight people and one leader. This seems an ideal-sized group to me. The last couple of week-long backpacks that I have led have been this size or smaller and it is much easier to keep a small group together.

For these trips I applied for a wilderness permit for ten people. You don't have to supply the names of the people in your group, which you might not know in advance, anyway. The wilderness permit is issued in the leader's name or that of whoever applies for it. This practice gives me a solid base against being pressured into accepting more people than I want. If someone nice really insists on coming along, I can always tell him or her, "Gee, my wilderness permit is full, but if you can get one of your own in Lone Pine (or wherever), you're most certainly welcome to come along!"

Then you either hope that they *can* get a permit at the last minute, or that they *can't*, depending on how nice they really are.

To show you the wide spectrum of advance information that a trip leader can and should send to the participants in an organized backpack, here is what I sent to those I led on a recent four-day trip in the southern Sierra Nevada.

The roadhead for this leisurely family-type backpack in the Cottonwood Lakes and Mt. Langley area is the end of the Horseshoe Meadow Road. This branches south from the Whitney Portal Road a few miles west of Lone Pine, where last-minute supplies and gasoline are available.

It is recommended that you drive up on Wednesday, to become better acclimated to the elevation. There is an unofficial campground across from the Cottonwood Pack Station (indicated as a sawmill on the old USGS topo), about 12 miles up the Horseshoe Mdw Rd. Outhouses and stream water. Look for the Orange Crate VW van (704 HFU) back amongst the trees.

Thursday we will leave a car or cars at the Cottonwood Lakes trailhead a mile up the road for our return. We will drive another mile up to the road-end at 10,000 feet. The first day's backpack is about 5½ miles, first along Horseshoe Meadow, then up switchbacks to Cottonwood Pass. Slight uphill on to Chicken Springs Lake (also called Chicken Fat Lake, and other similar names). Wood scarce, so no campfire.

Friday we continue up the Pacific Crest Trail (which we joined at Cottonwood Pass), past Siberian Pass below and to the west, to a junction with the Army Pass trail. About a mile along this we camp at the junction of this trail (which goes on to Upper Rock Creek) and the trail up to old and New Army Passes. Beautiful spot. Good fishing at Rock Creek Lake, etc. Wood plentiful, so campfire.

Saturday we go up the Pass trail for about four miles to old Army Pass. Anyone opting to climb Class 2 Mt. Langley can split here. Up some switchbacks to the top of New Army Pass (12,400 feet), from where Class 2 Cirque Peak can be scrambled. Down into the Cottonwood Lakes Basin, with camp at Long Lake. Wood scarce, heavy useage, so no fire.

Sunday out to the cars at the trailhead. About seven miles this day, but almost all downhill. Everyone can head for home, or for a motel and a swim in Lone Pine. The Dow Villa Motel is our favorite, with a second-floor room facing west for the sunset over Mt. Whitney and the Sierra Crest.

Bring lug soles, Ten Essentials, of course. Only barbless flies are allowed at Chicken Fat Lake. No fishing in the Cottonwood Lakes. Faint chance of evening rain. Maybe bugs, so bring repellent. Shorts during the day, longies at night. Stoves. Tent or tarp a good idea.

If any last-minute questions, call me Tuesday, at 788-7080, between 9 a.m. and 3 p.m.

Single-spaced, this fit on one side of a sheet of typing paper. As you can see, it contains a great deal of information on how to get there, what to expect, and what to bring. A few minor changes were made during the actual trip due to circumstances which could not be anticipated. The Long Lake campsite was bypassed in favor of a lower site, due to unexpectedly high winds. I had camped at both locations, so knew this minor change was a wise one.

The reason that I no longer lead organized backpack trips, such as this, is not that I'm unwilling to take the responsibility for the other people, but that such a trip is overly-planned, overly-rigid, and overly-repetitious, by necessity. I increasingly prefer to walk the mountains on my own, setting my own pace, and spending the nights wherever it suits me to do so.

I strongly believe, however, that if you are new to backpacking, you should go out as a member of an organized trip several times to pay some of your dues. Solo backpacking without the experience necessary to be properly wary is highly dangerous. You are often very far away from physical or medical help. If a local outdoor club offers a course in backpacking and/or survival, by all means take it. Check with the adult education division of your local colleges. If none of these are available, at least thoroughly read several of the books listed in chapter 17, particularly *Mountaineering: Freedom of the Hills, Medicine for Mountaineering,* and *Hypothermia: Killer of the Unprepared.* Then go on a couple of group backpacks.

When you finally feel reasonably confident in your knowledge and your abilities, lead a couple of easy group trips yourself. See what *that* side of the coin is like; you may be surprised. Then, and not before then if you have good sense, try solo backpacking. You may find that you are your own best friend or, perhaps, your own worst enemy.

When you do decide to go it alone, as a part of your awareness, be sure to leave a photocopy of your wilderness permit and a schedule of your plans with a friend or relative. If you have none who are convenient or trustworthy, leave this information at the ranger station or sheriff's office nearest your starting point. They can't find you if they don't know where to look, and, more importantly, if they don't even know that you're missing!

This is also the reason for signing any trail registers you may pass. If you don't come out of the mountains when you were supposed to do so, at least the rescuers will know where you have been and can limit their search area.

Always, always check out with whoever you left your schedule with. It makes the authorities very angry to search for a lost backpacker for several days before discovering that he is at home, watching TV. And it can be very expensive for the irresponsible backpacker!

# 3

# Boots, Socks, Shorts and Hats

Over the last ten years or so, manufacturers have come out with a wide variety of special mountaineering and backpacking clothing. The reason is the same as is the manufacturing of special clothes for skiing and yachting: profit. Current catalogs show down jackets at $75 to $120, parkas at $60 to $170, wool knickers at $50. Boots have truly gone out of sight, with standard mountain climbing boots selling for between $65 and $115, with heavy-duty expedition boots at $145 and up. So what to do?

The weird idea that you *need* special clothes to go backpacking, or mountain climbing, reminds me of recently meeting a woman I hadn't seen for about a year. We were exchanging chit-chat on what we had been doing since we had last met, when she mentioned that she was "into running."

My interest perked up, and I asked: "How many miles do you run a week?"

She smiled. "Oh, I'm not *running*. I'm just 'into running.' Why, I don't even have my outfit yet!"

Most experienced backpackers, who are horrified at the increasingly rising prices, do as they always have done. They do not buy special backpacking and mountaineering equipment, except where there simply is no other choice. Certainly you almost have to buy a lightweight backpack, a warm and compact sleeping bag, a weatherproof shelter of some kind, and light and reliable mountain stove. But $120 for a down jacket, and $170 for a parka?

I'll tell you what I carry in the way of clothes for a spring-summer-fall trip into the Sierra Nevada, and then you make your own decisions. I'll be camping at anywhere from 10,000 to over 12,000 feet elevation. I'm not expecting rain or snow, but I want to be ready for them. Temperatures at night may drop to freezing, though rarely, and below freezing even more rarely.

During the day I will usually wear shorts. These may be any of several pairs I have in the shorts' drawer at home, although the most-comfortable and most-practical seem to be the Scout Leader khaki shorts I bought at a store selling BSA uniforms. Men's BSA shorts currently sell for about $15, women's for about $18. This is a bit expensive, but they are very rugged and should last for many seasons.

In average mountain weather I wear my normal jockey shorts and a cotton fishnet top. The newer models of these fishnet undershirts have solid fabric shoulder sections, so your pack straps won't push the netting into your skin. The air space between the netting provides a layer of thermal insulation between your body and your shirt. I find this keeps me cooler in the summer and warmer in the winter.

Over this fishnet undershirt I wear a long-sleeved shirt. Most mountaineering authorities don't recommend cotton shirts, as they can be very cold when wet, and offer almost no airspace insulation in themselves. Still, they can be very comfortable in hot weather, and don't take up much space in your pack. Ideally, any shirt you use for backpacking should have long sleeves, as wind and temperatures can change rapidly and temporarily on the trail, and the same is true for the amount of heat that your body is generating. The easiest way to remain comfortable on the trail is by rolling your sleeves up, down, partway up, opening a few front buttons, closing the front. It soon becomes almost automatic and, under most conditions, saves having to put on and take off parkas and sweaters. The long sleeves, even on a cotton shirt, allow you to play the microclimates by ear. A short-sleeved shirt or a T-shirt doesn't.

If I'll be at high elevations for most of the trip, say above 10,000 feet, I prefer to wear a long-sleeved lightweight wool shirt. I prefer a Pendleton, but there are undoubtedly other fine brands. Just make sure your choice is ruggedly stitched. A light wool shirt such as this is rarely too warm in the thin, clear air of the high mountains, particularly with frequent adjustments to the sleeves and front.

For boots I wear the least expensive I can find that fit the needs of backpacking. I read the ads in backpacking catalogs and magazines for mountaineering boots with wide-eyed fascination and envy. But I don't buy the climbing boots they offer, at from $65 to $115. Many beginning backpackers, and some who should know better, do.

I'm not going to be doing high-angle mountain climbing.

I'm not going on an expedition to scale Annapurna.

I'm not going to solo the North American Wall.

What do I need with mountain climbing boots? I'm going backpacking in the mountains, most of the time on reasonably good trails. I don't need three or more pounds of specialized boot on each foot. With three pounds for both boots, I can be ever so much more comfortable . . . physically and financially.

For example, my current boots are a pair of lined Wayfarers, from Recreational Equipment, Inc. (REI). See the list of suppliers' catalogs in chapter 17. I bought them for about $25 a couple of years ago; they now sell for $35. They are high-topped walking shoes, which I need; they are not impressive-looking Everest boots, which I do not need.

Other sources of reasonably-priced boots are Sears, Wards, Penney's, and Red Wing. Don't shop for mountain boots which are automatically over-priced, but for high-topped work shoes. These are made to be comfortable in the field and to last. Many now come with lug soles, which, for our purposes are almost essential. Surplus Vietnam jungle boots can be bought for $15 to $20 through military surplus dealers. Check the catalog of P&S Sales, listed in Chapter 17. They have lug soles, screened vents in the arch, and canvas tops that can be cut down to a more comfortable six-inch height.

Almost all serious backpackers, and some humorous ones, wear thick "Ragg" wool socks. This is largely a matter of tradition, so experiment with various sock combinations until you find what best suits your feet and your boots. Your feet are of critical importance, as they are what will get you into the mountains, and out again. The standard package is to put on a pair of lightweight cotton socks with the heavier wool socks over these. I almost invariably do so. I have few if any complaints, and almost never have a blister.

I have read that rinsing your feet with denatured alcohol is good for them and will toughen them. I tried it once or twice and couldn't tell any difference except that I had one more thing to carry and to spill in my pack. Foot powder is also a good idea, I guess, to absorb moisture and to lubricate the foot-in-boot. I always intend to take a can along, but I rarely do.

Do I buy custom-made boots? Is that why they fit so well? No, the last three pairs have been purchased by mail, two from REI, the other from L.L. Bean. I didn't use any special break-in technique, as recommended in several backpacking books. I just put them on and started wearing them. But I do wear medium-thick cotton athletic socks with thick wool socks over these. I always carry moleskin in my first aid kit, but don't have to use it over hot spots or blisters more than once or twice a year. Then it's almost always my own stupidity for letting a sock wrinkle and not taking the trouble to re-adjust everything when I first feel something going wrong inside my boots. I break in the new boots to my feet and my feet to the boots, by wearing them around the house and around town for several weeks before I wear them in the mountains.

The other clothing items that I'd be wearing on this mountain backpack trip would be a pair of dark glasses and a red felt hat. The glare off snow can be literally blinding, and even off light-colored granite it can be painful. It's so much more pleasant to wear dark glasses. Neutral grey lenses are the best, as they don't change the colors of nature, which is one of the reasons that I'm out there in the first place.

A red felt hat? Well, not all backpackers wear red hats, or any hat whatsoever, but I wear a red one. Each spring I buy a new red "crusher" hat from L.L. Bean, REI, or one of the other suppliers. Currently they sell for $4.95. They're made in Germany, can be rolled up and stuck in your pack, and the sweatband falls apart after a couple of wearings. Why the sweatband is not made of a more moisture-resistant material I cannot fathom, but it is not.

*South of Forrester Pass in the Sierra Nevada*

Why red? They do come in other colors. Visibility is the key word. While most of my backpacking gear is dark-colored to better blend into the background, I want at least one item that can be seen a long way off. If you are leading a group, it makes it easier for the hikers behind to keep you in sight. With all the solo backpacking I do, I want that rescue chopper pilot to be able to spot me. It's part of planning ahead to avoid getting into an emergency situation in the first place. Also, if you shoot color film, a red hat adds a sensational touch to mountain photography with its preponderance of grey rocks, blue sky, and dark green foliage.

To carry my love of the red hat one step further, why wear a hat at all? A lot of supposedly knowledgeable mountaineers and backpackers don't. I know that a hat protects my head from too much sun and from excessive heat-loss—both apt to be troublesome at high elevations. The head, with its enormous blood supply, can radiate the blood's heat at a fast clip. Okay, a base-ball cap or a beret should prevent this, but I don't find these brimless caps comfortable, and I look like a ninny wearing them. A felt hat with a brim offers adequate protection against heat-loss and heat-gain, plus having the brim to shade my eyes against low-angle sunlight, the campfire's glare, and rain and hail.

Now, there is one problem with a felt hat such as I'm recommending. The air around your head, inside the crown, cannot escape. This is fine in cold weather, but a hot afternoon on a steep trail will stew your hair and the top of your head. I punch a series of quarter-inch holes around the crown, about three inches apart and about halfway up the crown. If I can't find my tent grommet punch, I cut diamond-shaped holes with an X-acto knife.

After losing several mountain hats complete with club pins and other memorabilia, I found a simple way to rig a chin cord that wouldn't get in the way when not under the chin. First I tap in a small metal grommet on each side of the hat where the crown meets the brim. These are the size grommets used for shoelace holes in shoes and boots. You may be able to get this done at a shoe repair shop.

A bola tie cord of cloth or leather is just the right length for a chin cord. Try a rock shop or lapidary supply dealer for these. Bola tie cords come in a wide variety of colors. They have plastic tips similar to those on shoe laces. The metal tips you may have seen on bola ties are cemented to and over these plastic tips. The bola cord can be tied out of the way most of the time, and fairly quickly remounted for use under the chin with a simple overhand knot above the brim holding the chin loop in place. It can be adjusted by slipping the overhand knot up or down the bola cord.

With the clothing that I've told you about so far, I'll get along just fine during the day on the trail. How about in the evening, when I'm camped at 11,000 feet, and the temperature drops as though I were camped at the terminator on the moon? Is that when I sneak out the $125 goose-down parka that is squirreled away in my pack? No, no, a thousand times no—for several reasons. Down is expensive. Down is worthless when it gets wet. It turns into non-insulating knots. A single jacket or parka doesn't give me the flexibility of warmth and comfort that I want. As the evening temperature goes down—and it does very rapidly above 10,000 feet—I first put on an old and much-repaired camel's hair sweater. As it gets colder or if a night breeze comes up, I add another layer with a nylon wind parka I always carry. The parka has a solid front, a hood, and comes halfway down my thighs.

As the afternoon wanes and the evening waxes, I've also traded my Scout shorts for long pants to keep from freezing my knees. I often see backpackers huddling around their sorry little campfires, in great puffy down jackets and daytime shorts, and I feel no sympathy for their shivering and mosquito slapping. A pair of long pants doesn't take up much room in my pack, nor weigh much, and the evening comfort is worth it. In the summer these may be an old pair of khakis. They're more to cut the inevitable down-canyon wind than for heat insulation. If I suspect colder evenings, I carry a pair of woolen knickers and some high wool socks. I bought these years ago because I thought they made me look more like a real mountaineer. I wouldn't buy another pair, though. They're up to $50 a pair, the high wool socks offer no protection against mosquitos and gnats, and I've given up trying to look like a real mountaineer.

With my multi-layered, inexpensive clothing, I can stay comfortably warm in the cold night air. If it gets too cold, I can always crawl into my sleeping bag. A pair of surplus U.S. Army wool gloves are very nice to have along, too. Mittens are warmer, but make it more difficult to light pipes, hold wine glasses, or perform other essential tasks.

Many of the hiking shorts sold today in sporting goods stores have an elastic waistband. These are quite comfortable, but make certain that you bring a belt if your long pants require one. On a week's backpack in the Sierra Nevada, where I started out wearing shorts, I forgot the belt. The long pants in my pack were an old pair, which had fit well when I had several inches more of waistline. Trying to hold up your pants with a piece of nylon tent rope is really a drag.

If I were to buy an insulated jacket or parka, I'd most certainly buy one filled with either Dacron Holofil II or Fortrel PolarGuard. These synthetics are almost as light and compressible as down. They have the great advantage of losing

*Trail Camp, at 12,000 feet, on the Mt. Whitney Trail*

very little of their insulating airspace when wet. The water can actually be wrung out of them, which is not true of down.

After a day on the trail, it is a simple pleasure to be able to take off your sweaty boots and to slip into something drier and lighter. This is also the ideal time to rinse your feet and change into cleaner socks. A pair of light moccasins or shower clogs may be comfortable around the campsite, but what if something should happen to your boots? I have never had anything happen to mine, but just suppose yours fell into the campfire, or a porcupine ate them, or a bear stole them . . .

what would you do then? A secret fear of being bootless in the boonies is the reason I carry a pair of jogging training flats for camp shoes. They are as lightweight as any rugged shoe you could buy. They are reasonably compact and, if runners can do marathon distances and more in them, they will certainly get me out of the mountains in an emergency.

I wore these training flats on a three day backpack to over 10,000 feet to see if this really were true. I wore only the cotton athletic socks that I normally wear for running. The shoes felt comfortable and light, but there was one hazard: being low-cut, running shoes do not cover your ankles. This could be a minor disadvantage to some people, but I found that in walking down-hill I repeatedly kicked myself in the ankle—a grazing shot with the rough edge of the sole. I had idly wondered why there was an oddly-polished area over the ankle bone on my high-topped boots. This was the reason, but with the high-tops I had never noticed it before. If you have trouble kicking yourself in the ankle, you can try taping them with moleskin or injecting them with Nembutal, although I haven't tried these methods.

The important thing in planning your clothes for a backpack trip at anytime of the year is to imagine the worst conditions that might occur. Summer in the Sierra Nevada should be warm and safe. After all, didn't John Muir call it "the gentle wilderness?" But storms sweep up from Mexico and the tropical Pacific with unpredictable suddenness, and they can catch you far back in the mountains. A few extra pounds of foul-weather clothing may just save your life, even in the sum-mer, and certainly will add to your peace of mind.

I always, and I mean always, have a light nylon rain poncho and rain pants handy in my backpack. In the occasional minor rain showers of an afternoon, I rarely bother to put them on, but I have them with me, just in case.

What extra or replacement clothes should you have with you? Backpackers who pride themselves on travelling super-light don't carry any extra clothes or almost none. I have heard of people taking along one spare sock—not a spare pair—one sock. Each evening they use it to replace the dirtiest of the two on their feet and rinse out the one removed.

This would seem to be stretching weight-saving a little far.

After all, how much does a pair of socks weigh? Now, you don't need two extra pairs. On a long backpack trip you're not going to stay very clean anyway, so the best plan is to try to stay as evenly dirty or semi-clean, as you can.

Carry a couple of clothespins. The miniature plastic ones sold for plane travel are about as small and as light as you could wish. Every evening or two rinse out your used socks and underwear. Soap and detergents are pollutants, so try to use neither. Rinse everything away from the stream or lake, squeezing water through the material. Due to the brain's ability to adapt to gradual changes, everything will appear miraculously clean after each rinsing—until you compare it with really clean clothes when you get to the motel or home. The difference is horrifying!

In the interest of cleanliness and comfort, but not of weight-saving, I usually carry two extra pairs of jockey shorts, and two pairs each of cotton inner socks and wool outer socks. This way I can change into dry and relatively-clean things each evening and yet only have to do rinse-laundry every second night. Dirty, sweaty socks are not as warm in the sleeping bag as clean, dry ones. If you're too lazy to do occasional rinse-laundry, you can rationalize that it's the dryness of your sleeping socks that keeps your feet warm, not the cleanliness.

If your nose runs a lot, handkerchiefs can pose a problem. White city handkerchiefs very quickly become quite unsightly, so large bandanas are the best solution. They come in dark reds and blues, so dirt and grime aren't as noticeable. Their large size makes them ideal for many other tasks: face towels, dish rags, pack strap padding; face mask for robbing stage coaches. Tie two corners together, put the bandana on your head under your hat, and you have a Foreign Legion sun shield for the back of your neck.

One time, when I broke a wrist in a fall, I used a bandana for several days to bind it in place of the elastic Ace bandage which I had forgotten to replace in my first aid kit. Obviously, the bandana can be a very handy item.

# 4

# Packs and Frames

There are many difficulties in selecting the best backpack for your particular needs and we shall explore a few of them. The most obvious feature to catalog browsers is that backpacks are becoming increasingly expensive, along with everything else. You can get along without an expensive tent—by using a tube tent or a tarp, for example—but it is just about impossible to backpack without a backpack. This means from $50 to $125. The good side of the story is that your backpack should last for many years. With reasonable care there is nothing on a backpack that can wear out. I've had my current REI pack for seven or eight years, and the only sign of wear that is in any way threatening is a fraying of the tiedown straps. If they ever were to break, they could be replaced quite easily.

You should send off for the equipment supplier's catalogs listed in chapter 17 and read over the sections on backpacks. There are quite a few manufacturers and a wide variety of models. The models themselves may be offered in three bag sizes or configurations, and the aluminum frame to carry the bag may come in three or even four sizes. The catalogs will tell you how to order the proper frame size for your build based on things like your height, or at least the distance between certain parts of your back.

The big decision comes in selecting the bag itself, and the major point in question is the volumetric capacity of this bag. The amount of weight that you can carry in your backpack is largely up to you. Volume is a different matter. Many of the items that you would like to carry on a trip are not heavy, but they are bulky. They take up space, and that's what you may not have unless you select your pack with care.

Before a trip I always pack and repack several times, trying to work out the best arrangement for the many things that I'm going to be carrying. First I put in true necessities: food, survival gear, tent, sleeping bag, and so on. Then comes the problem of fitting in a huge pile of things that I would like to take:   down booties, extra shirt, Japanese noodles, paperback, hockey puck. I know that within a few days the volume of the food will be less, leaving a little more space, but it just isn't available at the start.

I'll mention a couple of ways to get around this lack of space a little later, but I want you to note its importance early on. In comparing different models, check their capacities. The catalogs almost always give this, usually in cubic inches. You don't need to try to visualize it, just use it as a numerical comparison. Make a list if you want, then you can note that this particular volume is about average, this is less, and this is more. My personal recommendation is to buy the largest capacity bag available for the size frame that fits your body, if you plan anything beyond easy weekend trips. Having a large bag three-quarters filled is much more pleasant than having a small bag with twice as much gear as will fit into it.

Almost all backpacks sold today have nylon bags suspended one way or another from a frame of aluminum alloy tubing. The complete empty rig will weigh three to four pounds. The major improvement in recent years has been the use of a wide, padded hip belt, attached to the lower part of the frame. What this does, and where it is such an improvement is to shift most of the weight of the pack off the shoulders and onto the hips and behind, directly over the large and powerful leg muscles. The shoulder straps are used for little more than to balance the load.

In buying a backpack, first read the descriptions in the catalogs. Make a preliminary selection and eliminate those that are obviously unsuited to your needs. Then, try to inspect the ones left on your list at a sporting goods store. Don't count on the clerk in the store knowing anything of value about the backpacks he sells. He may well consider golf to be a vigorous outdoor sport. So have your decision narrowed down to a couple of choices. Your final selection at the store can be based on such factors as color, workmanship, and price. The sales clerk may be a backpacker, true, but even if he is it is rather unlikely that he has tried every model of backpack. And even if he has, what is that to you and to your particular needs?

Really, the only sensible advice that I can give to you is to pick the backpack that you think will be the best, in the color that you like, then learn to live with it . . . and from it.

I won't go so far as to say that all backpacks sold today are well-made. Any backpack that you buy through a major supplier or a reputable sporting goods store should last you for many years, however, if you take care of it. Obviously it will not do so if you drop it, fully loaded, and bend or fracture the frame.

This is the difficulty when you have to ship your backpack somewhere. On a bus it's best to stand right there, with a cold and sinister eye, as the pack is being loaded and unloaded. With planes, you can't watch. Your pack disappears through a hole in the wall. It is in the hands of God and the baggage handlers. One form of protection might be to wrap the whole pack and frame in padding of some sort. But what are you going to do with the padding when you get to your destination?

On a trip I helped lead a few years ago in Mexico to climb the major volcanos, one man from New York paid for an additional seat on the plane so that he could keep his backpack alongside him. Expensive and perhaps overly cautious, but he arrived with his pack intact and undamaged.

We mentioned backpack colors awhile back, and the importance of this should not be overlooked. Not only will you be happier with certain colors, but they should be determined by your purposes and attitudes in backpacking. On climbing expeditions, or in areas where there is a high-risk factor, it makes good sense to have your backpack and other equipment in bright colors—reds, oranges, and yellows. In an emergency it could well save your life. If, on the other hand, you will be strolling around the mountains, trying to be as inconspicuous as possible, then try to buy a pack and tent in dark blue, dark green, or brown.

*Bullfrog Lake from Kearsarge Pass in the Sierra Nevada*

I've noticed many times how much easier it is to see a group of climbers heading away from you than it is to see them coming back. The reason is simple: going away you see the bright colors of their packs, returning you do not.

Along with your backpack, you may want to carry a smaller day pack for short excursions away from your campsites. If you plan an afternoon hike of this nature, the slight additional weight of the day pack is well worth it. It's so handy to set up the tent, shove in the Ensolite pad and the fluffed sleeping bag, hang the big pack from a tree limb where it's safe from predators, then wander off with a light day pack.

In this day pack I would always carry the Ten Essentials (see chapter 12), camera, sweater, wind parka, water bottle, Sierra cup, and perhaps a snack or two. After the 40 pounds or more of the backpack, the five or six pounds of the day pack is like a feather! My hands are free, yet I've got everything with me that I need for a short hike to an intriguing pass or to a nearby peak. And I *could* spend the night bivouacked in safety, if not in comfort.

The factor that will actually limit how long you can stay on the trail backpacking is the weight of your load, not its volume as such. Your clothes and essential equipment—your "hard goods"—will weigh the same for either a short or a long trip. This means that the limiting weight is your food. I find it impossible to get my pack weight, with my hard goods, below 25 pounds. If I do, it usually means that I've left something out. With the best of weight-cutting, but with the safety gear and comforts that I feel are essential, my pack will weigh between 45 and 50 pounds setting out on a seven to nine day backpack. On my first nine-dayer, some years ago, my pack's beginning weight was 64 pounds. I soon learned to economize.

Since the length of your trip will depend on how much you can carry, how do you know how much is how much? Various authorities claim that you should be able to carry from 20 to 30 percent of your own weight with reasonable comfort. Norman Clyde, a Sierra backpacker and mountaineer of the 1920s, is reported to have regularly carried packs weighing 75 percent of his weight, and was once checked out with a pack weighing 88 percent of his weight. Clyde was an amazing exception, and I would advise you to start out with not over 25 percent of your body weight the first few times. Load the essential gear into your bag, then start adding food until you reach your weight limit. That's how many days you can travel comfortably, so plan your trips around that length of time.

You can extend your backpacking range by several methods. Having a chartered plane fly over and make air drops might

*Upper Rock Creek Lake, near Army Pass, in the Sierra Nevada*

prove a little too expensive, and certainly would be ostentatious. As discussed in chapter 9, take freeze-dried and dehydrated foods, assuming that there is an adequate water supply wherever you'll be hiking.

For summer-long trips you can plan restocking points near the trail, where either someone can deliver new supplies to you or you can have a package waiting for you at General Delivery. This is the only practical way to complete the longer trails in one session: the Appalachian, Pacific Crest, or Continental Divide.

If there are two or more people in the group, you can save weight by not duplicating several mutually-used items: tent, stove, pots, camera, rod and reel.

If you like to fish, you may want to add the weight of a rod and reel. Try one trip without them first to see if you have enough energy left after a day on the trail to fish for your dinner.

Many modern pack frames have open-ended tubes for the sides, so that a "frame extender" can be slipped onto and into the top, making it possible to lash additional gear on top of the pack bag.

On occasions where I have had too much to fit inside the pack bag at the start, I put the light but bulky items—sweaters, extra socks, etc—in a large plastic garbage bag. This I tie atop my backpack. Then, as the food supply shrinks, I can get the bulky objects into the pack one by one where they belong. The plastic garbage bag also makes an inexpensive cover for the whole pack to keep out either rain or small varmints.

As with several other of the "necessities" of backpacking, I don't really think that the particular make or model of pack you choose makes a great deal of difference. What is of importance is making your choice, then getting out on the trail. The pack is a means to an end, not the end itself.

Walking through and over the mountains is the end!

# 5

# Sleeping Bags, Pads and Pillows

The three most essential and most expensive items that you will need for backpacking will be your boots, pack, and sleeping bag. Just after World War II you could buy surplus U.S. Army Mountain Troops sleeping bags, down-filled, with an inner mummy bag and an outer square-cut bag, for $30 complete. But then the OPA, the Office of Price Administration, was phased out ("Prices won't rise; they'll just stabilize," we were told), and the price of down sleeping bags has continued to climb ever since. There are ways around the high cost of down, however.

Remember that a sleeping bag does not and cannot supply any heat. All the heat that you will ever have inside a sleeping bag is supplied by your body. The sleeping bag's purpose is to provide an insulating layer around your body so that its heat will not escape to the surrounding air, nor to the ground beneath you. Cold as such doesn't exist. Cold is a lack of heat. If you are not properly insulated, your body's heat will escape, and you will feel cold. No more, no less.

The best way to supply this insulation, with a minimum of weight, is to use a confined air space with a more-or-less airtight outer shell to retain the heat that your body generates in its normal functioning. Wool supplies this kind of insulating airspace, which is why wool sweaters and gloves are "warm." But wool is heavy and bulky for a given amount of insulation, so isn't used in today's backpacking sleeping bags. Before World War II you didn't have any choice.

Sleeping bag weights now, and with much better insulation, run from three to five pounds. With the collapsability of down and the synthetic fibers, this lightweight bag can be stuffed into a cloth container perhaps a quarter of the size of an equivalent wool bag. Wool bags are cheaper, but they are really only practical for car camping where you don't have to carry them on your back. I still occasionally see a backpacker on the trail with a huge wool bag. I always wonder if it's due to expense or inexperience.

Looking through the catalogs of the suppliers listed in the back of the book, you will see a bewildering display of down and synthetic sleeping bags. My last check showed goose down bags from $125 to $250, with an occasional duck-down bag at $110 or so. Down does have several fine points beyond the fact that it's "in." Down will recover and fluff up more than any other material currently used to stuff sleeping bags and jackets. This means that a down bag can be collapsed into a smaller stuff bag for carrying, yet will spring back into shape and provide more air space or loft when removed from the stuff bag. Therefore, a down sleeping bag is the warmest per pound of weight.

There are several bad points about down. Down bags are expensive, for one. There have been some scandals in recent years about down bag manufacturers diluting their down with chicken feathers beyond the government's stated limits. I feel that the critical failing of down is when it becomes wet it loses as much as 80 percent of its loft, and so offers almost no insulation. Synthetics such as Dacron Holofil II and Fortrel PolarGuard will only lose about five percent of their loft when wet, and can be wrung dry, which down can't.

Trying to dry a wet down sleeping bag inside a two-man tent during a storm is something I don't even want to contemplate! But for expedition climbing, at altitudes of 15,000 feet or so where everything is extremely dry, down bags are wonderful.

The synthetics are a little heavier and bulkier when stuffed, but not all that much. They certainly have several things in their favor. A quick scan of the catalogs shows a price range of $22 to $120, with $60 as a mean. In our mention of price ranges, the higher prices are usually for "expedition" equipment, for use in sub-zero conditions on high peaks. The lower end of the price range is usually nearer our backpack needs.

To me the most important quality of the synthetic-filled bags is that they can get soaked with water, be wrung out like a huge dishrag, and will regain almost all of their loft immediately. You can climb right in; you may be damp, but you'll stay warm. Perhaps I'm overly wary in my survival thinking, particularly as most of my backpacking is in the relatively rainless Sierra Nevada, but I can never escape the thought of spending a freezing night in a wet and useless down sleeping bag. If I owned a down-filled parka, which I don't, that would probably be wet and useless, too. And all it takes is one unexpected downpour, or a misstep crossing a creek.

I should mention, too, that people with allergies sometimes have trouble with down. The synthetics are non-allergenic and will not mildew as will down if left damp for awhile.

The most-important factor in the price of a sleeping bag, within any single fill material and style, is the temperature range in which it is considered adequate for protection. This used to be stated in all the ads in the catalogs, but I haven't seen this done lately. The price goes up as you buy more insulation or more loft which is understandable. But how much insulation do you need? This is the critical decision here, and the one you must make before you make any others. The decision will be based on the physical conditions that you will encounter in your backpacking.

If you will be backpacking only in the summer, you don't need a sleeping bag with sufficient loft to keep you warm at minus 30 degrees. The majority of my backpacking is done in the later spring, summer, and early fall in the Sierra. It gets near freezing at night camping at 10,000 to 12,000 feet as I frequently do, but it seldom gets below freezing. I carry a mountain tent on the colder trips, and this adds five to ten degrees of insulation. When it does get cold, I sleep with varying layers of clothing on. Why waste all the insulation or loft that I have so arduously carried in on my back? Why not use it as part of the sleeping bag's insulation, saving weight in the bag itself.

What do I carry as a sleeping bag, based on my multilayer

philosophy? Well, some years ago I went on a commercial trip to Mexico as second assistant leader and cook. We were to be camping from 12,000 to 15,000 feet on Popocatepetl, Ixtac-cihuatl, and Orizaba, and a down bag capable of protection at those altitudes was required. There were no equivalent synthetic fiber bags on the market at that time. I rarely use the down bag anymore, as it provides too much insulation for my normal trips into the Sierra Nevada. I frequently had to sleep half in and half out to vent off some of my body heat.

The sleeping bag that I've been using for the last four or five years is a $25 Dacron Fiberfil II tapered model that I bought, if memory serves, from Recreational Equipment by mail order. I have never had a cold night in the Fiberfil bag, including ones down to five degrees below freezing. On cold nights I always wear the next day's clean cotton and wool socks to bed, I keep my long pants on, but I almost always take off my sweater and windbreaker. I've thought of wearing wool gloves and some sort of hat to bed to help conserve my body's heat, but I've never gotten around to doing so.

My next sleeping bag buy, again from REI, will be a Dacron Holofil II model called an "Olympic," which sells for $21.95 in the current catalog. There is nothing wrong with the old Fiberfil II bag. It's just that I'm getting a little bored with it. After I run it through the washing machine, I'll pass it along to my 13-year-old son, who is still using the down-filled Mexico bag.

Many people, including me, find it almost impossible to sleep without a pillow of some kind. Sleeping on my side, as I prefer to do, I need something to raise my head enough to keep my neck reasonably straight during the night. A stuffed pillow would take up too much space to be practical for backpacking, although I have known people to bring them. I have found inflatable pillows too unnatural. As I'm getting into the sleeping bag, I wrap the running shoes that I have been wearing around camp in the sweater I have just removed. This I place in the bottom of the sleeping bag's stuff sack, roll up the surplus material, and I have a soft, cylindrical pillow. In the morning, or for an emergency during the night, I know exactly where my sweater and shoes are—under my head.

One problem with keeping your body heat inside any sleeping bag, regardless of the filling material, is that your weight crushes the bottom fill decreasing the loft. At one time the answer was to carry an inflatable air mattress but they were heavy. You can now buy lightweight coated nylon air mattresses that cancel out that weight objection. One worry is that when you have an airtight flexible container filled with air under pressure due to the weight of your body, leaks can occur. This means you must carry a small repair kit. No sweat, but the time at which you are most apt to discover a leak is in the middle of the night in the dark. Repairing a leaking air mattress in the warm sunshine is a snap; crouched in a cold tent, it is not.

Another deficiency of air mattresses is that they can be cold when you are sleeping on cold ground or on snow. The air inside the mattress loses its warmth to the ground, circulates around in there, and your body passes its heat on to the cold air. But in warm weather they are comfortable!

The answer to all this lost heat is another triumph for modern synthetics: Ensolite. This is a foam material, with the tiny bubbles within the foam separated and unconnected. This trapped air or gas makes the transmission of your body heat through the Ensolite almost negligible. Most of the Ensolite sleeping pads sold today are three-eighths of an inch thick, although thicker ones are available. The pads come in full-length and three-quarter length.

The price of Ensolite pads has gone up in the last few years, now to $12 to $13 for a full-length pad, so many backpackers are using the newer closed-cell polyethylene pads, which are less-expensive (under $5), lighter by at least half, and should work just as well. Some people simply can't sleep on any of these thin pads. I rarely have trouble with them, and will try the new polyethylene material, now that I have noticed the difference in price and weight.

Given that you have a sleeping bag that is warm enough, and under it you have an Ensolite or a polyethylene pad—what next? Well, if you're sleeping in the open, a small ground sheet is handy. Moisture will come up from the earth during the night, and you may slide off your Ensolite pad, getting your sleeping bag damp. With the closed-cell pads, you'll stay dry as long as you stay atop the pad. Inside a tent, the tent floor takes care of this.

When you select your sleeping location, naturally you avoid

*Sleeping bags are usually strapped to the bottom of the backpack. The mountain is 14,042-foot Langley above the Cottonwood Lakes Basin, Sierra Nevada*

the major rocks and stumps. Remove any pine cones, pebbles, and deer droppings. But now comes an important operation—and one I frequently forget until I am already in the sack—digging a hip hole. You eyeball where your hips and fanny will spend the night, then scrape away an area about a foot square, to a center depth of three or four inches. The actual depth is a matter of trial, and will depend on the dimensions of your protruding parts. Without this hip hole, it's like trying to sleep on a lumpy pool table. Horrible! So dig that hip hole first, before you get the tent up on top of the spot where it should be.

Even with a hip hole, adequate sleeping bag, and all the rest, I sometimes am extremely uncomfortable the first night or two on the trail. The ground fits my body quite well, but my joints ache. I toss and turn, trying to find a more comfortable position. It's probably more due to the change in physical conditions than to anything wrong with them.

Another thing that can add to this discomfort is a mild case of diarrhea, again more than likely due to changes in food, water, and exercise than to anything pathological. If I've anticipated both of these night problems, I'll dig into my medical supplies and get out some half-grain Emperin with codeine, aspirin, and Lomotil. A single codeine tablet with an aspirin will subdue the body aches for most of the night. The codeine has a limited but definite effect of drying up the trots but the tiny Lomotil tablet usually completes the job.

# 6

# Stoves and Campfires

Before we get into the subject of stoves and cooking, let's settle the question of whether or not we actually need to cook on a backpacking trip. Hot food is nice, but is it necessary? I've made a number of two-day and three-day backpack trips where I carried nothing but cold, ready-to-eat food. I find that I can do quite well, and be quite happy, with chocolate breakfast bars in the morning, and cheese, salami, and French bread for lunch and dinner. And I've saved the weight of the stove, its fuel, a pan or two, and a spoon—plus the trouble of cooking, which can be a drag when you're by yourself.

This simple fare might get monotonous on a longer trip, but it could be varied with dried fruit, powdered drinks such as Tang, and with gorp.

Gorp, if you haven't run into it, is a backpacker's accumulated hash of trail snacks. You can buy commercial gorp at backpacking stores, but it's not the real thing. To be right, gorp has to be accidental. You start out the season by mixing candy and nuts in a cloth bag, then add to it anything tasty that comes along: raisins, sunflower seeds, jelly beans. It's a standard backpacker item (if such a mishmash can be called "an item") for trail snacks during the day. It is a concentrated, high-energy food, and often looks ghastly.

The problem with cold meals for more than one person is

finding foods that everyone mutually admires. This does not seem to be as easy with cold foods as with hot ones. I happen to like cheese; my son abhors it. Luckily he does agree with my other favorites, such as Danish salami. This is a mild, lightly-spiced salami, so is easier to eat in quantity than the hard, highly-seasoned Italian salami. French and/or sourdough bread keeps well, particularly if you buy dinner rolls or small loaves. You can easily carry a plastic, screw-top, large-mouth container of oleomargarine, jelly, or peanut butter for variety. Chocolate bars are great for desserts or snacks, particularly those with nuts and fruit in them.

On a short backpack you're probably going to have at least one meal at the car camp before you start up the trail, as you do on most backpacks. Make this an elaborate meal, really cooking up a storm on the two-burner Coleman stove you carry in the car. When you come back out, you will usually drive to the nearest town for a meal. So, with the few meals that you'll be eating while actually backpacking, particularly on a short trip, you aren't going to die of boredom eating cheese, salami, and French bread. John Muir used to spend weeks in the Sierra Nevada with a lot less variety than that, and he had enough strength left over to found the Sierra Club.

And think of how light your pack will be!

On a longer trip, I'm not sure how this diet would work out, but I mean to try it on a week-long trip sometime. If you wanted to add a little variety, you could take along a rod and reel to catch an occasional trout. You could roast the fish over a wood fire, using a "backpacker's grill," or propping them up on sticks as they teach the Boy Scouts.

But let's advance on to the idea that you want to have hot meals, or at least a cooked dinner every evening. What is the minimum of additional equipment you will need? In general, backpackers have given up the idea of campfires for cooking or for warmth. The land needs the downed wood for nutrient more than we need it for a fire. We can cook much more easily and efficiently on a modern backpacker stove than over a fire. We can get warmth from our clothes.

If you check through the catalogs of the equipment suppliers, you will find that there are quite a few varieties of stoves on the market. We will immediately discount such toys as Sterno and heat tab stoves. They should only be seriously considered for use on day hikes, where you might want a lightweight stove to make a cup of soup or coffee.

That leaves us with stoves using kerosene, white gasoline, and canned propane. Kerosene is the safest, as it is not very volatile. It is difficult to ignite (as compared to gasoline), and easy to extinguish. Due to these safe characteristics, a kerosene stove must be primed with something easier to ignite: alcohol, gasoline, or an inflammable paste primer. This is a bother, but may be the only practical answer to anyone who is afraid of gasoline's explosiveness, or going into an area where kerosene but not white gasoline is available.

Modern mountain stoves using sealed cannisters of liquid propane are almost as safe to handle as kerosene stoves. This type of stove needs no priming, but can be difficult to start at extreme altitudes and/or at very low temperatures. In the type of backpacking that we are apt to be doing, neither of these should present any problem.

The one bad feature of these stoves is that you have to carry the fuel in sealed metal cannisters, which are heavy. When empty, you must carry the cannisters back out of the wilderness. There is always the problem of how much fuel is left in a sealed cannister, and how many spares you should carry. These are some of the reasons that I have always used a white gas stove, of the Svea-Primus-Optimus type. That, and the fact that I grew up with them.

The white gasoline stoves are the most efficient in their heat per ounce of fuel. I haven't tried all the variations available and so can only speak from personal experience. For lightweight trips, and solo trips where I plan to cook, I have a Svea 123R, which weighs one pound two ounces empty. This weight includes the windscreen and the top cover which is also a small cooking pot with its separate handle. This model is also called an Optimus 123R, as both Svea and Optimus (and I believe Primus) are made by the Optimus Company of Sweden.

For trips with more people involved I frequently switch to a Svea 111B. This model weighs several pounds more than the 123R, but it is extremely stable and reliable. It comes in a steel case, which makes it less subject to upsets when cooking in the snow, where the stove's heat can cause uneven melting.

The differences between these two stoves are relatively minor, but could be an important consideration for a particular trip. The 111B has a built-in pressure pump, so it is easier to prime (with its own gasoline). The 123R must be primed by hand with an eyedropper. Because you can pump pressure into the 111B after it has been primed and is lit, it will put out a great deal more heat. It is truly like a blowtorch and just about as noisy. But then, the 123R has a built-in windscreen, which might make it more reliable above timberline. As with so many things in life, you have to make your choice, then learn to live with it. So read all the catalog descriptions before you buy. With today's stove prices between $30 and $50, they are not the minor investments they were a few years ago.

Many, but not all, modern gasoline stoves come with "self-cleaning" generator tips. This means that by turning the fuel supply knob all the way on, a little steel wire pops up through the very small hole in the tip of the generator, which can become clogged with soot and impurities in the fuel. For this reason, never use pump gasoline of any kind, not even non-leaded. Buy either white gasoline, or the Coleman types of stove and lantern fuels sold by the gallon in sporting goods and hardware stores.

In priming a mountain stove, you ignite some alcohol or gasoline in a little pan around the base of the generator, the gizmo that sticks up out of the fuel tank, with the actual burner on the top. This priming heats the generator enough to vaporize the liquid fuel within it. This vaporized fuel is what is burned, with a cloth wick inside supplying more liquid fuel to the generator. With the addition of a pressure pump, as built into the 111B, you can neatly squirt the priming fuel through the tip and later force fuel in at a faster rate than wicking alone can do.

If your stove does not have a self-cleaning tip, you must carry Svea tip cleaners with you. A tip cleaner is a short piece of steel wire on a thin sheet metal handle, and it can get lost easily. It is easier to carry a small adjustable wrench with a couple of new or reconditioned tips taped to the handle. It is much easier to screw on a new tip in the waning daylight than it is to push a tiny wire through a tiny hole.

My Svea 123R has a self-cleaning tip, but it does not have built-in pressure pump. The two choices for priming without a pressure pump are to carry a medicine dropper to remove a little fuel from the stove's tank, or to warm the tank until it develops sufficient internal pressure to force a little of the fuel out through the generator tip. This last technique can be one of the horrors of beginning an otherwise perfect day. Few things can hold the cold like a brass fuel tank filled with gasoline. Trying to warm it with your hands results in painfully cold hands.

Colin Fletcher, who wrote *The Complete Walker,* saves his tea bag wrappers each evening, then builds a small fire with them in the morning in a small pit under his stove's fuel tank. Scraps of toilet paper will work, too. It is much easier, however, to prime with an eyedropper or you can buy a screw-in pump for a pumpless Svea-Primus-Optimus. But that's one more thing to buy, and one more thing to carry.

If you use a gasoline stove, always remember that gasoline can be dangerous. It is very volatile and very flammable, so handle it with caution. Never carry it in glass or thin plastic containers; metal fuel cans are strong and are inexpensive. Don't let children light or fill any gasoline stove. Never light the stove inside a tent or indoors; it may flare up as the priming heats the generator. Always light the match before turning on the fuel supply, and always do so with your head off to the side, not directly above the stove.

If your stove runs out of fuel while you are cooking, let it cool off for at least five minutes before refilling it. The best idea is to peer inside each afternoon after you have set up camp and fill the tank about three-quarters full. If you make it too full there won't be enough air space for pressure to build up satisfactorily. Checking each afternoon this way, you should always have enough fuel in the stove for cooking dinner and breakfast.

Always read the instructions carefully with a new stove and try it out at home (outdoors, of course) before you take it on a trip. I made one eight-day solo backpack with my new 111B Svea, muttering at it for not giving off enough heat, for cooking too slowly. When I got home I read the instructions and found that I was supposed to pump it again, after the priming pumps. I felt like an idiot.

I've always thought that one of those disposable butane lighters should be handy for lighting stoves and campfires. So far they either don't work properly or I lose them the first day. I worry, too, about becoming reliant on a mechanic gimmick like that, and then having it fail. Wooden matches, those old stand-bys, are not much better on a backpacking trip. Only about one in four lights at all, and then goes out again in the slightest breeze—and in the mountains there always seems to be a breeze. So, after much consideration, I carry many packets of paper matches. As I visit a lot of bars in between backpack trips, I always have a good supply, but you can also buy them by the box at most grocery stores.

Open up each packet, and let it roast in the sun for a half hour to get thoroughly dry. Then put two packets each into two-by-three-inch Ziploc bags. If you can't locate any Ziploc bags this small, try rock shops and jewelry stores. Paper matches are smaller and lighter than wooden matches, they light easily, and the plastic bags containing them can be distributed throughout your pack. This way there is very little chance of more than a few of your matches getting wet.

The amount of cooking gear that you will need depends on how elaborate your meals will be and for how many people you will be cooking. For one, two, or three people, I carry one two-quart aluminum kettle with a bale on top. It originally had a bracket on the back for inserting a metal handle, but I lost the handle, so I cut off the bracket to make it easier to pick up the pot with a pot grabber. These little aluminum gadgets are very handy. Without one you have to use your bandana for insulation when picking up a hot pot, and you usually end up trailing a corner of the bandana through the food.

But one pot or kettle should be enough. Cook in sequence, with the foods that dirty the pot more coming later along the time line. Start with soup, then Japanese noodles, finally the messy stew or whatever for the entree. This way you only have to wash one pot per meal.

If you're backpacking alone, you don't even have to carry a plate or bowl. Eat everything out of the cooking pot. A large spoon is all you need. You have a pocket knife, or should have. Anything that can't be managed with a knife and spoon can be picked up with your fingers.

Try to keep everything as simple as possible. Certainly it's fun to look at all the special equipment made for backpackers.

Catalogs are my favorite dreambooks. But don't buy anything that you really don't need, and don't take anything a second time that you didn't use the first time, other than your survival equipment.

As we have mentioned elsewhere in this book, most ecologically-minded backpackers believe that campfires are rarely justified in the high country. Wood is scarce and backpackers too numerous. A nightly campfire is indeed pleasant, but it is a tradition left over from an earlier time that we can no longer afford. I vary my practice, dependent on the country I'm camping in, but I try to have a campfire no more often than every three or four days—say two on a week's trip—and then only where downed wood is overly-abundant. This is another of the reasons that I have given up leading group backpacks. There almost always is some clown along who is miserable without a roaring campfire every evening.

So, if you want to join the ranks of ecologically-minded backpackers, carry a self-contained stove. Use it for all of your cooking, and forget about being a pioneer cooking over a wood fire. It scars the land and blackens your pots. Pack out all the unburnable trash. Better yet, pack out even the burnable trash. It won't weigh that much. Leave your temporary homes in the mountains cleaner and more pristine than you found them. No one should be able to tell that you have passed that way.

And if you must have a reason for cleaning up the wilderness, beyond your love of the earth, remember Somerset Maugham's statement that "The greatest satisfaction in life comes from doing a good deed in secrecy, and then having it discovered by accident."

Smokey the Bear may be watching!

# 7

# Tents, Tubes and Tarps

There are probably more opinions about shelter for back-packers than about any other phase of the sport. In the mountains you will see backpackers with nothing more than a plastic ground cloth to sleep upon. At the other extreme you will see them erecting elaborate tents suitable for a party of six on the west ridge of Mt. Everest. Your decision as to what type of shelter to carry will depend on many things: expected weather, insects, weight of equipment, number in group, cost, and your personal preferences.

Some, like writer-backpacker Colin Fletcher, have a hatred of tents, claiming that they "cut out the beauty of the night sky." They also cut out the beauty of rain and snow, not to mention the beauty of insects.

The super-lightweight school of backpackers carries a six-by-eight rectangle of thin plastic, weighing only a few ounces, to place under their Ensolite and sleeping bag. In the case of a light rain at night, they can crawl under the plastic and stay reasonably dry, if somewhat tense. Whether or not you can get away with this degree of abandonment will depend on the local weather and the state of your nerves.

At the other extreme are the fancy tent carriers. The advantages are security against bad weather, a barrier against mosquitos and other insects, and five to ten degrees more insulation against the cold. The possible disadvantages are increased weight and increased cost.

A look at the tent section of the suppliers' catalogs will boggle your pocketbook. These days $100 will get you what would appear to be the bare minimum, and you can pay $300 for the best, with another $50 tacked on for the necessary rain fly. Plus tax and shipping.

The ideal tent, as it is made today, and which is far from ideal, is to have the fabric of the tent such that it is windproof, yet will allow the moist air from your hot body to escape out through the fabric. Otherwise this body moisture is apt to condense on the inside of the tent, making things a little messy. However, if the tent fabric can breathe properly, it can't prevent the rain from coming in, defeating the prime requirement of a mountain tent. Until someone figures out how to eliminate the breathable-yet-waterproof dilemma, you also have to buy a special "rain fly" to rig up over the tent to keep the rain out. Ridiculous.

First off, forget about the $200 and $300 tents. They're for expeditions and the like, at extremely high elevations, and under the worst possible weather conditions. The added strength means weight, and a tent such as these may weigh eight or nine pounds, with another three pounds for the rain fly.

There are some more realistic mountain tents for about $100, complete with rain fly. If your backpacking is going to be in areas where rain and other bad weather is highly likely, or assured, you will need a tent of this type. A two-man version will weigh about eight pounds complete.

Can we beat the high cost of shelter? Certainly, and you don't have to risk your tired body on a little plastic ground cloth, either. The catalogs lovingly show the expensive tents, with four-color illustrations. Stuck away at the end of the tent section you will often find the bright solutions.

I have used two somewhat-primitive types of shelter for the last half-dozen years, and one of them is a "coated nylon" tent. The more expensive tents that I have just told you about are made of uncoated, rip-stop nylon, which is why they need a coated nylon rain fly in order to keep out the elements. My two-man tent looks identical to any other mountain tent, but the top, sides, and bottom are both windproof and waterproof, not just the floor and lower sides as on the expensive tents. My tent has mosquito netting and coated nylon flaps at the front, and large netted vents front and rear, to make up for its lack of "breathability."

In minor Sierra Nevada storms it has never leaked. In a thunderstorm on Mt. Shasta that lasted for several hours, it did begin to leak in one small area, but this occurred after four seasons of use, and with no maintenance. I later sprayed the leaky area of the tent roof with fabric sealer, and now hope for the best. True, this tent sometimes does have a little moisture condensed on the inside of the roof in the morning, but rarely and not much.

This tent probably wouldn't be worth much in a real storm at 15,000 feet, but I don't plan to be there anyway. Why did I buy this free-standing super tube tent in the first place? Well, curiosity for one thing. Another reason was the low weight of three pounds and four ounces complete with end poles, ground pegs, cords, and carrying bag. There is no rain fly because the whole ruddy tent is a rain fly! The cost? I bought mine for about $25 locally. A look at the new REI catalog shows what appears to be a duplicate for $32, which seems about right inflationwise.

The shelters that we have been talking about so far have a common advantage. They are all free-standing, which means that they come with metal or fiberglass poles or wands that support the structure. This makes it possible to sink the tent pegs and erect the tent into the ground or snow or to hold the tent ropes down with rocks. If you are going to be camping above timberline, as we backpackers often do, a free-standing type of shelter is almost a necessity. Almost, but not quite.

The next step downwards in cost, weight, and complexity is the coated nylon tarp. These can be pretty fancy, with all sorts of cute little Boy Scout tabs sewn at various points, and at $50 for an 11 x 13 footer. The other backpacking shelter that I mentioned using in recent years is a 9 x 11-foot coated nylon tarp, with no tabs but with small brass grommets at the corners and at the midpoints of the sides. This weighs two pounds and two ounces, and currently sells for about $30.

I carried this tarp on a nine-day backpack that took me over 13,777-foot Trail Crest pass, 13,200-foot Forester Pass, and 11,823-foot Kearsarge Pass. I camped at elevations up to 12,000 feet. It rained one evening, but I stayed dry and snug, particularly when camped in trees, where I could easily string my nylon

*A campsite in a Sierra meadow near University Peak*

parachute cord from the two corners that formed the roof of my
vee-on-its-side shelter. With the center grommets of the 11-foot
side pegged down, this left me a flat ground cloth 9 x 5½ feet,
and a sloping waterproof roof of the same dimensions. When it
rained, I slid further back into the protected vee. A hole or a
tear can be repaired with rip-stop nylon tape, or, in an emer-

gency, with a piece of the adhesive tape of the end of a Band-Aid.

Admittedly this configuration wouldn't be too successful in a violent storm, but I wasn't expecting one. If there had been a severe storm, I would have pegged down the tarp in a more secure vertical vee, pup-tent style. I would have it sideways to the wind, with one end closed.

Above timberline the rectangular tarp is not so practical. There just aren't many things around that are high enough for your roof support lines. If you have enough cord, 100 feet or so, you can run long support lines over high boulders, with rock weights at the ends to hold everything together. Such a shelter may leave much to be desired in a bad storm, but it sure beats standing around in the rain.

The ultimate shelter from the standpoint of economy has to be the plastic tube tent. These are cylinders of very thin polyethylene plastic, usually a hideous green color, and they weigh about two pounds. The "one-man" version is nine feet long and three-feet three-inches in diameter. Forget this one unless you are a midget. The "two-man" is still nine feet long, but has a four-foot nine-inch diameter. This means that you can put on your boots sitting up, without endangering your spinal column.

There are a few inconveniences to tube tents, but the current price of less than $8 for the two-man version can make up for quite a few minor sins. As with the flat tarp, you need a couple of high things to tie the support line to. The tube is held up by a rope or cord running from one high thing to another. It hangs on this line like abandoned laundry, your sleeping bag and Ensolite pad forming the floor and holding the floor down. Searching for the ideal pair of trees at each campsite can be maddening.

The chance of moisture condensing inside the tube tent is about the same as with a coated nylon tent: a possibility with which most of us can live. You must be certain never to close off both ends of a tube tent, however, as the polyethylene is both waterproof and airproof. It's quite possible to suffocate, particularly if you're dumb enough to fire up your little Svea for some late night cocoa. You can seal the ends part way, though, with wooden, spring-loaded clothespins.

Once, at 12,000 feet on Mt. Whitney, I had a one-man tube

*Coated nylon tarp set up between four trees to give backwall*

tent set up between some boulders when a giant thunder-rain-hail-lightning storm swept in. With the small diameter one-man job, I couldn't sit up or even move around easily. The wind blew through the tube like a wind tunnel. The rain water ran down the sides of the boulders in one end of the tube and out the other. It was like living in a sewer filled with ice water.

Generally, though, a tube tent will keep you dry and warm in moderate rainstorms. The one thing that it cannot do, nor can an open-faced tarp setup, is keep out mosquitos. If there are mosquitos in the wilderness where you will be camping, a tent with netting is almost a necessity. Without netting the only recourse is to douse yourself with insect repellent before going to bed. This may keep the mosquitos from actually piercing you, but you still have to put up with their flying around inside your ear all night.

What would I recommend, then? Well, if the weather of your backpacking area will allow it, I'd start out with a tube tent. Then, after trying this for awhile, switch to a $30 coated nylon tarp or tent. Watch what the other backpackers use, and ask them about their opinions. Spend at least a season on the trail before deciding whether or not you want to spend a hundred or two on a really good all-weather tent.

There is no question that, given certain physical and financial conditions, a well-made mountain tent is essential to comfort and safety. But, will those conditions have very much to do with your style of backpacking?

# 8

# Setting Up Camp

There are two basic philosophies in deciding where to camp while backpacking. One type of backpacker likes to keep walking until late in the day, and then simply pick the best spot available. The opposite extreme is to keep hiking until dark, then fall down wherever you might be. I've only done the latter once, on a 19-mile day, and I don't intend to do it again.

The method I adhere to most of the time relies on planning ahead by studying topo maps and sometimes reading trail guide books. I say to myself, "Today I will have no major passes to cross, so I should be able to cover the mileage from here to that lake in five or six hours. That should get me there about three in the afternoon, and I'll have plenty of time to set up camp, try to catch a trout or two, and be ready for bed when it gets dark (and cold)." Generally this works out quite well.

This pre-planning does have two weak points, in opposite directions. Until you get used to mountain backpacking there is a great tendency to overestimate the distance you can travel in a day. You read about people doing 20 miles, so you figure you should be able to do 15. At least at first, forget the tiger bit. You're a mile or two above your normal oxygen supply, you have 30 to 50 pounds on your back, and you may not be in as fine a physical condition as you like to think.

The other weak point in pre-planning your camping spots is that you may arrive at your campsite so early in the day that you are tempted to put in another half dozen miles. I have rarely experienced this feeling myself, but I'm willing to accept that it might happen to others.

Regardless of which method you use in selecting your camp for the night, there are several things to be considered when you arrive there. Pick the location primarily on the basis of nearby water. This can be a lake, or better yet, a fast-running stream. Don't camp right alongside this water. To avoid any chance of pollution, it is best to camp at least 100 feet away from it.

Some people have trouble sleeping with a stream rushing by too near their tent. Many insects favor damp places. Streams run along the lowest part of the terrain, and that's where the cold and heavy night air will likewise flow. Ideally, then, find a flat and level terrace that is a hundred yards from the lake or stream, and fifty feet or so above it. I have read many times that there are fewer mosquitos at these higher sites, but have never seen any proof of this. In most mountain areas, you just have to learn to live with mosquitos during much of the back-packing season. After all, they were there first.

Many backpackers take off their packs the minute they reach their camping area, and then walk around looking for the best sleeping spot. I always keep my pack on, as I hate having to put it back on again later when I have located my campsite for the night. Decide what is best for you.

In looking for a spot for the night's camp, you should search for several things simultaneously. You need a level area large enough for the tent and kitchen. A flat rock for the stove, and to sit on, is a dividend. Are there some trees that will shade you from the glare of the afternoon sun? How about a reasonably clear shot of the rising sun? You'll appreciate its warmth at six in the morning. No matter which way the wind is blowing now—although it is usually up-canyon during the day—where will it come from during the night? Which way should you face the tent? As a general statement, night breezes are down-canyon, though not always.

Having dropped my heavy pack, my first chore is to get enough water for the afternoon, night, and morning. A collapsible plastic water jug, with a spigot, is invaluable for this. I now carry a 1½-gallon "Fold-a-carrier" that cost under $3. Be sure you buy one with a handle, and with thick walls. Trying to carry one of the thin plastic models without a handle is like trying to carry a giant amoeba.

Even in a deep stream or lake, it is almost impossible to fill a plastic water jug by submerging it, particularly if you are hanging onto a nearby rock with one hand to keep from falling in. First, try to find a place where the stream creates a minor waterfall. Even then, the easiest way to fill the jug is with a plastic drinking glass or a Sierra cup. It is a monotonous process, but it makes you appreciate how many cupfuls make up a gallon. Carrying the full jug back to your campsite up the hill, you also will appreciate how heavy water is, at "a pint's a pound, the world around."

The next thing we need to take care of is our shelter. In the chapter on tents and tarps, we talked about the relative merits of various types of shelter, so we won't go into that here. With your hip hole dug, and your shelter erected, shove in the Ensolite pad and the unstuffed sleeping bag. Unfold your pack and place various items into the front corners of the tent: flashlight, toilet paper, water bottle, the sleeping bag stuff bag as part of your pillow.

Now is the time to take off your boots and sweaty socks, and to change into cleaner socks and camp shoes. While we recommend running flats, anything will work that will protect your feet against small rocks and pine cones.

Where there are no marauding bears, tie a suitable rock to the end of a nylon cord about 25 feet long. Unsuitable rocks are much easier to find, but that is one of life's little challenges. Toss said rock over a tree branch eight or ten feet above the ground. This should be a simple task, but seldom is. Either haul up your entire pack or a bag containing all your food, so that it is four or five feet off the ground. At this height only a bear can reach your pack, but so can you when you need those last-minute things you forgot earlier. The pack or bag should hang a foot or more from the tree trunk, so that climbing animals can't easily hop aboard.

I forgot to do this once, when I was "only going to be away for a minute." When I returned, forty-five minutes later, a large marmot was enjoying the fruits of my labor. He (or she—I didn't ask, and haven't the faintest idea of how to tell) had gnawed holes in half a dozen food bags, and had finally settled

*Above timberline one problem is driving stakes into the rocks. This is at 12,000 feet on Mt. Whitney*

on a box of prunes, which saved me the trouble of having to eat them. But the effects of half a pound of prunes on a twenty-five pound marmot must have been profound.

There are many predators out at night that can climb into your pack if you leave it on the ground, and they can eat or ruin a lot of your valuable food. A plastic garbage bag tied firmly around your pack will keep out most of the smaller and less-ferocious ones. In bad bear country, like parts of Yosemite, the park service will explain to you what to do and what not to do. This is a specialized situation, so I won't go into defending your food against bears here. We'll assume that your backpacking will be unbearable.

Tie a length of nylon cord between two trees, give your old socks a couple of rinse-and-squeezes, and hang them out to dry overnight. In the event they aren't dry by morning, you can hang them through the straps on the back of your pack, to dry in the sun and the mountain air.

If you're carrying liquor with you, now is the time for your evening cocktail. The major trouble with liquor is that it's heavy and bulky. Beer and wine, with their low alcoholic content, are the most impractical unless you can afford daily air drops. A plastic water bottle full of pre-mixed martinis sounds like a possibility, but they turn out to be rather unpalatable fresh out of a warm pack. And you have to carry olives and proper martini glass.

Stream water is usually amazingly tasteless, at least to those of us who are used to the thicker, richer city water. I have tried scotch and light rum (not at the same time, you understand) with stream water, and neither was satisfactory. I've always meant to carry some 140-proof Myer's rum, but have not yet done so. Frank Ashley's *Backpacker's Rag* recently mentioned some new dehydrated drinks, including screwdrivers, and these may be a major breakthrough for backpackers. But at least up to now I've found drinking to be such a bother, and the "natural high" of the wilderness to be so effective, that I generally go cold turkey on the longer trips.

Someday marijuana may be legal. Being compact and light, it could be the ideal relaxant for backpacking, but since it is illegal at present, no one carries it, of course.

Before you settle down to preparing dinner, spend a couple of minutes wandering around the immediate area picking up other people's litter. Carry a medium-sized plastic bag for this purpose, and carry out all the cigarette filters, pop-top tabs, and aluminum foil you can. Perhaps, if you and I leave a litter-free campsite, the next person to use it will be ashamed to toss his debris around. I like to believe this is so, but I'm not really sure.

The question of whether or not to have a campfire is one that you must answer for yourself. Obviously you shouldn't have one at high elevation near timberline. The few trees here grow very slowly, and their dead leaves and branches are needed to enrich the mineral soil. It has been said that for every 100 feet of elevation gain, spring comes one day later and fall one day earlier. Above 10,000 feet, the growing period of summer can be very short.

Colin Fletcher, in his book *The Complete Walker* and elsewhere, has written against campfires with the objection that their glare reduces your night vision so that you cannot enjoy the beauty of the night sky. Fletcher, however, is an Englishman, without our American Indian and pioneer heritage of campfires. When you are camped in an area with plenty of downed branches, there is nothing wrong with gathering enough for a small Indian campfire. I read somewhere, "White man build big fire and sit far away; Indian build small fire and sit close."

In your mountain travels you will see some campers—and fishermen seem to be the worst at this—who burn huge logs, with flames shooting ten feet in the air. Perhaps they are terribly insecure in the woods. Frequently, I have unfortunately observed, they restart their campfire early in the morning—if indeed it ever went out during the night—and then leave it burning when they disappear down the trail. I have spent a fair amount of time, which could be better devoted to the trail, hauling water to douse these campfires. As with policemen, there never seems to be a forest ranger around when you need one!

The best way to find enough wood for your fire is to walk a hundred yards away from your campsite. Most backpackers just won't walk very far looking. Say to yourself, "If I were a lazy slob, where *wouldn't* I go to look for wood?" Then go there. This even works around heavily-used car camps.

Since backpackers will often car camp at the beginning of a wilderness trip, it's always a neat idea to have at least one night's firewood in your car. Scrap lumber and tree trimmings are great. If there should be an adequate supply at the campgrounds, you can always take your personal supply back home with you for another trip. Not having to scrounge for wood at your roadhead camp makes life much more pleasant.

On the backpacking part of your trip, however, try to keep your campfires small and few. If there is already a fire pit, use it, rather than make a new scar on the land. Before you crawl into the sack, make sure that your fire is out. Pour some of your water onto it, so there is no chance that a sudden night wind could blow sparks into nearby bushes or trees.

I haven't mentioned trying to cook over a wood fire, and I won't. The only reason that the Indians and the pioneers did it, in my opinion, is that the Svea-Primus-Optimus stove hadn't been invented yet. If you must play it primitive and cook over an open fire, read the Boy Scout "Fieldbook," which gives many suggestions.

In a little Sierra Club pamphlet, *The Care and Enjoyment of the Mountains,* Michael Lonhman gives the following procedure for lighting a campfire.

> First, clear a circle around your campfire site at least five feet in radius of any material that might ignite and spread the fire: pine needles, dried grass, leaves. Then lean one tiny twig against a large chunk of wood. Hold a match or a candle end under the twig, and place other small twigs in the flames as they grow. Build a four-sided fort or chimney of larger twigs and sticks around this center flame, once it is self-sustaining. Dry pine needles will help. In the rain you can do this under the protection of a tarp, making sure that you don't burn a hole in the tarp, of course. A small chimney fire such as this will keep going in a moderately heavy rain.

How late you stay up around the warm campfire will depend on your companions, your wood supply, the night temperature, and how tired you are. In solo backpacking I rarely light a campfire, as I have mentioned, and frequently I am into the tent and into my sleeping bag by the time the sun disappears over the ridge to the west.

On backpacking trips I implore you not to bring a portable radio. You are in the wilderness to see it and to hear it. Even when the volume is turned low—and few of the idiots who carry them ever turn them low—they can be heard for hundreds of yards. If you must have one with you, please be good enough to use it with an earphone.

In the morning some backpackers like to cook their breakfast while still lying in the warmth of their sleeping bags. This is both rather tricky, and could be downright dangerous to do inside a tent. If you really must have hot food or hot coffee first thing in the morning, you have my sympathy. I will lie in my warm sack, looking out through the doorway at the sunlight moving across the land, and eat the breakfast bar that I stuck in my hat last night. I have water or Tang in the plastic bottle right alongside me. When I do get up, I'm ready to stand around in the warm sunlight for awhile, then start packing for today's adventures.

Crawl out as gracefully as the limits of the tent will allow, and put on your boots and sweater. Refill your pockets with whatever you put in your hat last night. Put on the hat to keep the morning sun out of your eyes. Drag out your sleeping bag,

*It is pleasant to camp where you will get the early morning sunlight*

unzip it, and spread it out on a sunny rock, or hang it from a tree limb. The bag picks up body moisture during the night. Pull out the tent pegs so that you can flip the tent over to dry the bottom, if it is wet.

Now eat your breakfast while you stand in a patch of sunlight. Fill your water bottles from the bigger plastic jug, and dump the rest of the water on the ashes of last night's campfire.

Stuff your sleeping bag into its stuff bag, trying to be as lighthearted about this particular chore as you can be. Fold up the tent and repack it in your backpack. Then, toilet paper roll in hand, stroll to wherever your restroom is located. Coming back, make a final litter sweep of the area, picking up anything you missed yesterday. Make certain that you are not leaving any of your camping equipment hanging from a tree or behind a rock.

As you hoist your backpack onto your shoulders for another memorable day, there should be no evidence that you have ever stopped there. Fill in your hip hole; scatter pine needles over the tent clearing. Repair that small piece of earth that has been your home for the night. Satisfied that you and the earth are in reasonably good shape, give a last searching look, and start off down the trail.

But please don't sing as you walk. I may be around the next bend, listening to the wind.

# 9

# What's for Dinner?

We have written elsewhere in this book of the idea of backpacking without a stove, eating such foods as cheese, salami, French bread, candy, and the like. In this chapter, though, we will assume that you want at least one hot meal each day, and that invariably means the late afternoon or evening dinner.

First we must decide what to carry in the way of pots and pans. Unless a really major point of your backpacking trip is eating, you can very well get along with one pot or two at the very most. As your mountain stove only has one burner, you obviously can't cook more than one thing at a time. If you like after-dinner coffee, though, it can be handy to have a small second pot for heating the water before you clean your befouled main pot. A better solution is to heat the coffee water in your metal Sierra cup.

Looking through the catalogs and at outdoors stores, you will see a lot of cooking sets. Don't bother with them. They are too elaborate for your backpacking needs. All that you need is a two-quart pot, a pot lid, maybe a second small pot, a Sierra cup, and a spoon. You will carry a pocket knife, as part of the Ten Essentials, or should. Forks are for the overly-sophisticated; fingers are for backpackers.

Aluminum pots are light and dents in them are easily hammered out if you put your mind to it. I have read that stainless steel would be superior even though slightly heavier. With a tighter surface, stainless steel would be easier to keep hygenically clean. I have not seen any in the backpacker catalogs, however. The answer may be looking in normal kitchenware stores or restaurant supply stores rather than outdoors stores. It might take a little judicious hacksawing and filing to adapt the pot to our needs, but it may be worth the effort.

The difficulty of trying to cook "normal" foods while backpacking is compounded by the fact that with increasing elevation above sea level, the atmospheric pressure drops. With this, the boiling point of water drops, and cooking time increases, sometimes approaching eternity.

I remember one backpacking trip I went on as a kid, when I took along a box of regular white rice for dinner. We camped at not much above 7000 feet, and I put the rice on to cook. Two hours later it still wasn't done, but I ate it anyway. It tasted like hot BB's.

Not too many years ago the choice of lightweight foods was very limited. Most of the dehydrated foods tasted awful. Fortunately, freeze-dried backpacking food tastes much better today. Check the catalogs and your nearest outdoors store. You'll be astounded at the wide variety of meals that you can buy in little packets: beef stew with vegetables, chicken chop suey, turkey tetrazzini, beef stroganoff, turkey supreme. Freeze-dried dinners used to be quite expensive, but with the rising cost of fresh foods, they seem less so today. They cost about $2.00 to $2.50 for a "two-man" portion. Without the usual accompaniment of salad, soup, bread, dessert, a two-man portion will serve one person, a four-man two.

For most of your lightweight food supply, though, you can save a lot of money by shopping the supermarkets. A few years back there weren't many items there that were of much use to the backpacker. They were all either too complex in preparation or the cooking time was too long. It is also very difficult to get most backpacker stoves to stay lit with a low enough flame for simmering.

Read the instructions on the package to make sure that the cooking doesn't require a multi-stage production number with seven pots. You want to be able to do it fast and in one pot.

There are so many instant or near-instant drinks on the market these days at the supermarkets that what you take along is simply a matter of choice: iced tea mix, Tang, Kool-Aid.

"Electrolyte" drinks should be carried also. These "electrolyte" drinks, which contain sodium chloride salt plus some of the trace elements you lose by exercising are great for replacing lost body fluids. There are several commercial products designed for this purpose . . . ERG, Gatorade, Body Punch . . . and some are available in powder form, suitable for backpacking.

Here, however, is a recipe for a homemade electrolyte drink which you can, literally, make for pennies. This recipe is for one quart of water, so you can make up the dry ingredients in advance, and carry several small Ziplok bags with you.

| | |
|---|---|
| Ingredients | ¼-teaspoon Sea Salt |
| | ¼-teaspoon Lite Salt |
| Flavoring | ¼-cup sugar, or other sweetening |
| | 1 -teaspoon Tang, lemon powder |

The added flavoring is up to you, as is the sweetening. With a total of only half a teaspoon of salt per quart, the solution isn't going to taste all that salty. At least I don't mind it, although one friend I tried it on claimed that it tasted "like used sweat."

I carry a couple of small packets of this mix more as an emergency drink than for everyday use. In strenuous mountain climbing or backpacking you lose a lot of sodium in sweating, and potassium, calcium, and magnesium in urinating. This loss can result in muscular cramping and weakness. The Sea Salt and Lite Salt mix supplies these exuded elements.

You'll be less thirsty while you backpack if you drink at least three cups of water or other liquids at every meal. If you tend to be dehydrated easily, carry a Sierra cup, or a plastic cup, on your belt or backpack harness, and get a small drink of water everytime you pass or cross a stream.

Many backpackers come out of the woods badly dehydrated, which is just plain masochistic foolishness. With proper planning, you should end up back at the roadhead parking area with only your emergency water left; no more and no less.

Frank Ashley, in his January 1979 *Backpacker's Rag,* reports that the Global Marketing Co., of Portland, Oregon, is coming out with dehydrated alcoholic drinks. Named "Sure Shot," the alcohol is suspended in a powder that looks like a gelatin dessert mix. All you add is water. Retailing at $1.39 each, the first selection includes a vodka sour, screwdriver, and cappuccino with cafe de menthe. We haven't seen these listed in any of the catalogs yet and the problem of alcoholic beverage sales could prove a tricky one, but keep an eye out in your local backpacking and liquor stores. Dehydrated booze has been a campfire topic for many years. Perhaps there really are better things for better living through chemistry!

I have known some fanciful backpackers who, at least on overnight backpacks, take table linen and candelabra with them. This may be too much, but there is no reason that you can't carry a few fresh things with you.

Thick-crusted breads will last a week or more, if kept sealed and in your pack. Small dinner rolls are better than a larger loaf.

Fresh eggs can be carried in a special compartmented plastic container, sold at most outdoors stores. I have owned one for years, but have never used it. It's easier to break a few eggs into a wide-mouth plastic jar. The center of your pack stays reasonably cool, and you can eat the eggs your first morning in the hills.

Canned bacon can be a treat. You leave it unopened until you are overcome by an overpowering urge for a mess of rashers. On one nine-day trip I took along a three-pound slab of unsliced bacon. Each evening I cut off that day's ration, diced it, fried it, then added a freeze-dried dinner and some water.

Ham also keeps well, but both ham and bacon could prove hazardous to your health in bear country. I heard of a camper who carefully wrapped a half-eaten ham and stuffed it into the foot of his sleeping bag. Later that night a large bear answered his dinner invitation, and dragged him and his sleeping bag a hundred yards before he could eject. Never keep any food, not even a midnight snack, in your tent or sleeping bag in bear country.

In the Yosemite high country, the bears have learned to undo the old-fashioned rope-over-the-limb food caches, either by biting the tiedown end of the rope in half or by breaking the limb. The recommended bearproof cache is now made by throwing a rope over a quite high limb, pulling the food bag up to the limb, then tying a counterweight on the down rope. The counterweight is then pushed up with a long stick until it and the food bag are even.

*A wilderness camp in Montana. (Montana Department of Highways)*

The obvious question is how does the backpacker get the food bag down the next morning? If your stick is long enough, you can poke around trying to get one side low enough to pull down. A better plan is to loop a light cord through the food bag so that both ends of this cord trail on the ground. With these two lines widely separated, a bear is not too apt to pull both at one time—the only way the food bag will come down. At most the bear will pull down one half of the rope loop, pulling the other half after it, leaving the sly camper an interesting task in the morning.

While a little soap or detergent would make dish washing in the wilderness a great deal easier, they really aren't acceptable in the wilderness anymore. They pollute the soil, and they pollute the water. I carry a small pill bottle with some detergent in it, just in case. I don't end up using it once a season, but it can be invaluable when I really do need it. If you must use some soap or detergent, pour your soapy water into a hole in the ground at least 100 feet from the nearest stream or lake. Better yet, make it 200 or 300 feet away!

Finally, how much food should you take? You'll have to find this out by trial and error. The amounts and kinds of foods that you eat at home seem to have very little to do with the amounts and kinds of foods that you'll crave on a backpacking trip. My son and I both eat considerably less on a backpacking trip, which is very likely a major part of the reason that I lose ten pounds on the first trip of each season. Some backpackers make absolute hogs of themselves, scarfing down elaborate break-fasts, munching huge sandwiches at every rest stop, devouring four-man freeze-dried dinners in the evening, and finally disappearing into their tents clutching a two-pound Cadbury bar.

For several years I took too much food and carried half of it back to the roadhead. Now I plan the amounts a little tighter and include a bag with a pound or so of instant rice and some freeze-dried peas.

But then I don't go backpacking in order to eat. I go to see, to hear, to feel, to experience. I'd eat rocks if I were capable of doing so.

# 10

# Family Backpacking

If you like to backpack with a small group, rather than go it
alone, family backpacking may well be your best bet. You know
the members of your family well, which is more than you can
say for the members of any organized club trip.

But your family is different. If you can tolerate them at
home, the chances are that you can do so on a backpack trip.
Maybe not, but at least you're ahead of the game. A small
group, even just one other person, also makes for shared loads
and lighter packs. You don't save a lot of weight individually,
but even the few pounds from the divided-up tent, stove, fuel,
and pots can mean a couple of day's more food and an
extended range of travel.

At what early age can family members go backpacking? If
you'll settle for short distances each day, and a lot of extra carrying, you can start with tiny babies. The best source book on this
is Goldie Silverman's *Backpacking with Babies and Small
Children,* listed in more detail in chapter 17.

To be a self-supporting member of a backpacking team, able
to carry his or her own equipment, and perhaps a little of the
food load, I would say that a child should be ten years old. This
can vary, and I had planned to take my son Richard on his first
season's backpack trips when he was ten. But by nine he was
showing enough interest and enough hiking ability on local day
hikes, that I bought him his first mini-backpack that year. The
summer that he was nine, he backpacked everywhere I did,

including an eight-dayer that I led for the Sierra Club and a private father-and-son four-day backpack and climb of Mt. Whitney (14,495 feet) which I let him lead.

With a family group, you can let a child lead you, setting the pace, and not lagging far behind. This can be important, this joy of leading, and is why I would avoid taking a young child on an organized club outing, unless it was deliberately set up for families with children. The Sierra Club and others do have such trips.

I led one where a father brought along two eight-year-olds for their first backpack. While the father was a good local hiker, it was also his first backpack. He had a new mountain tent which he had never set up before. He had a new mountain stove which he had never tried to light before. One of his boys had a chest cold. They didn't like walking six miles in one day. They didn't like camping at 11,000 feet. It was a real bummer, and they turned back to the roadhead the next morning.

How old is too old to start? That would depend on one's physical condition, and one's desires. If you run or jog half a

*A family backpacking in Wisconsin*

*Fishing can be a family activity on a backpack trip*

dozen miles a week, you should have no troubles. If you don't, or can't, no matter what your age, you probably will have troubles. I know of two local hiker-backpacker-mountaineers in their mid-70's. From the end of my teens until I was over 40, I considered walking to the bathroom as more than enough exercise for any one day. Then, for some reason which escapes me now, I started hiking nearly every weekend, bagging the 5,000 to 11,000 foot peaks in the mountains north of Los Angeles. This, and the Angeles Chapter of the Sierra Club's Basic Mountaineering Training Course, led to backpacking. Now, at 55, my backpacking plans for the future are even more inclusive than they were when I was younger. Not longer, but more inclusive. At 55 I'm not a tiger, but then I never was.

Age, I should think, is of minimal importance. What is important is the desire to carry your home on your back for a few days or a week, so that you can walk and camp where few others can. It is also the desire to escape the noise and crowding of the car campgrounds. It has been said that the population density in the back country decreases to the square root of the distance from the nearest paved road, and to the cube root of the distance above it. Even with the large number of people backpacking today, this formula would still seem to be true.

Now, you're not going to be able to escape the outdoor idiots completely by going backpacking, but you certainly will see less of them. And, not being confined to a laid-out campground, you don't have to camp cheek-to-jowl with a group of oafs. If they won't leave, you can leave. With your family, you are a self-sustained unit, and can be as independent as the terrain allows.

When you take a child backpacking, it is a very good idea to allow him to bring along a favorite toy. The outdoors is unfamiliar territory, so a touch of home, beyond his parents, will be comforting.

Take along a Frisbee or a kite and string. Both offer wonderful possibilities for fun in a mountain meadow.

Take along fishing gear, and let your child try to catch dinner. Many or most states do not require children to have fishing licenses. I well remember son Richard's shout of glorious victory when he reeled in his first flashing Golden Trout when he was 11 years old. The next day he was willing to walk, in fact, he insisted on walking, 19 miles to the next overnight campsite.

I would say that he was quite impressed at having caught his first trout. So was I.

# 11

# How to Get There

I have told you a lot about the actual physical process of backpacking, but there still remains the question of how to get from your home to where you start backpacking, and how to get back when you finish backpacking. This can present some nifty problems.

The most obvious solution in this day and age is to drive your own automobile to the roadhead where the trail starts. This seems so simple, yet where do you leave your car when you take off up the trail? Will it be safe? How do you get back to your car if your planned route doesn't return you to the same spot?

You can lay out many backpack trips so that you do circle back to your starting point, but this is often impossible to do. How can you hike one of the great national trails—the Pacific Crest, the Continental Divide, or the Appalachian—and return to your starting point? The only solution would be to backpack a given distance, then turn around and backpack back. At first thought this seems a singularly dull way to hike a major trail, but it does have much to recommend it. First, you would be returning to your starting point and your car at the end of each leg. Second, travelling each section of the trail in both directions, you would certainly know and appreciate it more than with a single passing. It would take you at least twice as long to complete the given trail, but when you had finished you could say, "Not only have I hiked the entire Appalachian Trail [for example], but I did it twice, south to north and north to south."

You might be able to plan a trip so that you end up at a town from where you could catch a bus back to your starting point. This sounds great in theory, but very few backpack trips start from towns.

One possibility is the car shuttle which requires a small group with several cars. Everyone shows up at the starting point and pitches camp. Several cars are then driven to the end point, parked and locked, the drivers returning to the starting point in one of the cars. When everyone arrives at the end point a week or so later, the drivers whose cars are parked at the starting point are driven there, and return to the end point to sort out the assorted passengers and backpacks. This can be a little time-consuming in shuttling back and forth, but it sure beats most of the alternatives.

Here is the information that I mailed to the participants of an overnight in-and-back trip in the mountains north of Los Angeles. Here we did not need a car shuttle, although I shuttled some supplies to the turn-around point.

### Pacific Crest Trail: Mill Creek Summit to Messenger Flats

This is a very interesting backpack, but it is a strenuous one, and not for beginning hikers. The two miles up the north side of Mt. Gleason are on good trail, but are quite tiring that late in a 10-mile trip.

We will leave the Mill Creek Summit area (water, outhouses) at 8:00 AM on Saturday. Arrange your own transportation to this point. We can take no one. There is no water on this section of the Pacific Crest Trail, so carry at least two liters per person. We will take a comparatively slow pace, with frequent rest stops, and a lunch stop. We should reach Messenger Flats by 3:30-4:00 PM. I will have driven there the day before and secured a campsite (table and firebox), leaving some firewood, which could be scarce. Messenger Flats has piped water and outhouses.

Backpack in your sleeping bag, ground cloth, two lunches, one dinner, one breakfast. The Pacific Crest Trail is mostly on the shady north side of Mt. Gleason ridge, but the weather would call for shorts and T-shirts on the trail, longies for the evening.

Vegetation along the trail ranges from chaparral to grass and oak, pine, fir, and cedar. Elevations are from 4,750 feet at Mill Creek Summit, to 6,500 feet on Gleason, and 5,900 feet at Messenger Flats.

Take the Angeles Crest Highway north from La Canada to the Palmadale cutoff at Clear Creek Station. Turn left onto Angeles Forest Hwy. Or, come up Big Tujunga Canyon to Angeles Forest Hwy, and turn left onto it. At Mill Creek Summit, park on the left side of the road, just beyond the Mt. Gleason Road intersection, and across from the picnic area. We should be back to the cars before 3:00 PM on Sunday.

This may seem overly elaborate, but when I'm leading a backpacking trip, I like to give each participant all the information they could possibly need. Single-spaced, it easily fit one side of a page. Other leaders may send you more or less information.

I was assistant leader on one trip where the leader was an aerospace engineer. He sent everyone a beautifully worked-out trail plan, with every junction and key point listed to the hundredth of a mile, with elevations to the foot. The trouble was that he could not relate the actual earth to its representation on a topo map. We ended up camping at the wrong lake, and then he led us up the wrong route to the wrong peak.

A good trip summary does not mean a good trip; however, nor is the opposite necessarily true.

A situation where the basic car shuttle breaks down is one where the plan is to traverse an area with no fairly direct connecting roads between the starting and end points. An example would be an east-west crossing of the Sierra Nevada. To shuttle cars around this range would take hours, even days. The solution is to start two groups, one from each end of the trail. When they meet at midpoint, the drivers exchange car keys, plus a detailed description, and a map of exactly where the car is parked those many trail miles away. At the end of the trip, everyone drives to some place near home, switches back to their own car, and the great double-shuttle is over.

Is there a chance that your car will be burgled or vandalized while you are gone? Of course there is, but I've never had it happen, and I feel that the chances are certainly less in the outback than on most city streets.

Try to park in designated and signed overnight parking areas. These are supposedly patrolled by park or forest personnel, county sheriffs, and/or highway patrol. A thief is less apt to try to rifle your car where many are parked; there is too much of a chance of someone returning unexpectedly.

Before you leave, double-check that all doors and windows are locked. Roll the windows all the way up to make it more difficult for anyone to "coat-hanger" your door open. Don't leave anything of value in sight.

Okay, you've parked your car. It's facing downhill so that it will be easier to start should the battery be low when you get back. The wheels are blocked with rocks. You've locked the doors and checked them. Now you're standing alongside your pack with your wallet and your keys in your hand. What do you do with them?

I put mine in one of the zippered pockets in my pack where they are not going to be accidentally pulled out when I'm getting something else out of that pocket. Other backpackers hide them under a rock that they feel sure they can find again. I did have my wallet get soaked once by having it in an outside pocket on my pack, and walking through a short-lived rain storm. But under a rock it could have gotten just as wet, or stolen, or eaten by an animal, or some other horrid thing to worry about. I'd rather have everything with me, and only have to worry about my losing them.

I sometimes do hide an extra ignition key in a magnetic box up under the chassis of the van. I only remember to do this about once in six times, and then I worry that some clever car thief will think to look exactly where I put the magnetic box, and has already driven away and sold my van in Mexico.

If you take a car with you and plan to leave it for days and weeks, you've got your worries. No question about that.

On an organized trip, such as those put on by large clubs, the leader is the one who must figure out the type of shuttle that best suits the particular trip. Unless he then supervises every stage, things can go wrong. I led a Sierra Club trip a few years ago where I asked the participants to first meet at the end point roadhead, leave someone's car there, then come on to the starting point where I would be waiting. The trouble was that no one stayed at the end point for more than a few minutes and, seeing no one else there, quickly drove on to the starting point. We thus ended up with all the cars at the starting point, and no way to get back to them from the end point. All we could do was hike for three days towards the end point, turn around, and spend three days hiking back, which was not what I had wanted to do.

*Bullfrog Lake from Kearsarge Pass*

If you will be backpacking by yourself or with one other person, you could park your car in the town nearest your starting trail point, then hitchhike to it. If your trailhead is at the end of a well-used and paved road, this should work out quite nicely. Walk to the edge of town to be free of local traffic, then wait. I decided that I was above hitchhiking and would walk the 12 miles between Lone Pine and Whitney Portal one summer. As the sun rose higher, so did the temperatures. I had turned down earlier offers of rides and soon was cursing myself for having done so. The next offer, an hour after starting, I quickly accepted.

Having a child along can be very helpful, I found the summer Richard was ten, and we hitchhiked from Independence to Onion Valley. The ride offers came so quickly that I didn't even have time to tell him to try to look like an abandoned waif. Hitchhiking is a solution, or at least a partial one, if you are able to trust yourself to the kindness of strangers. For a lone woman backpacker, or even two women, I'm not so sure. I believe that there are fewer creeps out in the boonies, but then again, everything is so terribly remote. The subject is touchy; I'll not advise you here.

Another possibility, which we mentioned earlier in passing, is that of public busses. Greyhound and Trailways have scheduled runs all across the country. The backroad routes get the out-dated equipment, but this is understandable. Many of these runs are slow, stopping at every small town along the route, but they will get you there.

Check your local Greyhound and Trailways depots for schedules. Listed on them will often be the schedules of smaller bus companies which run connecting service back into the mountains. For example, there is a small line which runs a daily bus between Fresno and Yosemite Valley. Such service may not be every day of the week, nor all year long, so make sure you have your timing right. And there may be only one trip each day. Miss that and you may spend a weekend in Fencepost Corners.

You might be able to get from a town to the roadhead using a local taxi or shuttle service. These rarely are permanent busi-nesses and are difficult to keep track of. From time to time, however, some guy who lives in the town decides that he could make a little summer money by meeting the Greyhounds and shuttling people up the mountain. I've never tried these shuttle services, but I intend to do so. The best method of locating such a service would be to write the town's Chamber of Commerce. Not having the faintest idea of the C of C's correct address, I'd address the envelope:

> Chamber of Commerce
> c/o City Hall
> Fencepost Corners, Calif. 00000

Whether or not the same person would be willing to pick you up a week or so later, I don't know. It might be better to locate a second shuttle service operating out of the town nearest your end point. Naturally, you can expect better service if there are several people in your group, all paying so much a head.

For longer trips to the backpacking area, check into going part way by train, then switching to busses or other local trans-portation. The main advantage of busses is that they go to more places, and you are in more direct contact with your pack in the cargo section. For even greater distances, or where time is important, the airlines may be the best answer.

If you want all of these problems to be at their minimum, go with an organized group where the leaders shoulder all the responsibility. Clubs across the country, such as the Sierra Club, have dozens, even hundreds of trips each year. Some are free, some cost, some leadership is excellent, some leadership is awful.

Next up in having someone do the planning for you are the commercial trips run by the clubs. The Sierra Club, for example, had nine commercial backpack trips scheduled for 1979: two in Baja California, two in the Grand Canyon, others in the Superstition Mountains of Arizona, the Mt. Lassen area of northern California, Death Valley, Escalante Canyon in Utah, and the Navajo Indian Reservation.

The largest strictly commercial outfit for our sort of trips is Mountain Travel (see chapter 17 for addresses) which runs trips literally all over the world, from the Himalayas to the Arctic, from Tierra del Fuego to Mt. McKinley. These trips are graded from relatively easy hiking trips up to climbing expeditions on major peaks. The cost is high, but Mountain Travel can take you to those faraway and adventurous places that you'd never attempt on your own. The leadership is knowledgeable, and there is as much luxury as can be expected under the physical conditions of travelling to some of the most remote places on earth.

How to get there depends both on the physical nature of the available transportation and on how much responsibility you are willing to assume. If you consider that getting to and from the wilderness is part of the overall adventure, then strike out on your own. If you're not quite so sure, yet, then begin with organized club trips. If you're even less sure of yourself, or have simply become tired of assuming all the responsibility, then try one of the commercial trips.

Each will supply its own set of adventures!

# 12

# Mountain Medicine and Survival

Patient: "Doctor, it hurts when I raise my arm like this. What should I do?"

Doctor: "Don't raise your arm like that."

From which we paraphrase:

Reader: "What if I should hurt myself or get sick miles from a doctor. What should I do?"

Author: "Don't hurt yourself or get sick."

It is very true that few people go out of their way to injure themselves, in the mountains or anywhere else, but it can happen. A couple of years ago I made a silly misstep on a backpacking trip, fell, and broke my left wrist. I still blush inwardly when I think of falling off a trail. It wasn't an accident, it was an error in judgment, and a stupid one at that.

Most of us don't know too much about medicine and first aid. We assume that we are immune to such catastrophes, and that if the worst should happen, there will always be a doctor or a paramedic handy to take care of everything. While backpacking, this is extremely unlikely to be so. You will spend most of your backpacking time miles from the nearest paved road, and farther from the nearest town with a doctor. Therefore, your physical condition will have to depend almost entirely on your own caution, your own equipment, and your own knowledge.

First off, I would highly recommend that you take one of the American National Red Cross' first aid classes. The recently-adopted "Multimedia System" course is much less boring than the old one was. The information and practice that you will get may prove invaluable, it will give you more peace of mind, and important fragments of it will stick with you for years.

If you can't get to one of these Red Cross classes, at least buy a copy of the text *Standard First Aid & Personal Safety*, as listed in chapter 17. Two other books which I consider essential that you read, if not own, are *Medicine for Mountaineering* and *Hypothermia: Killer of the Unprepared*. Both of these are concerned with medical problems that are peculiar to the high country or at least are found there in more potent forms. Read through these three books so that you'll at least retain the basics of what to do in an emergency. Better yet, you may gain enough knowledge to avoid the emergency situation altogether.

Most books on backpacking contain a long chapter on first aid, usually cribbed from one or more of the above-mentioned books. We won't, as the original sources are much better. One of the best book chapters on the general subject of mountain medicine is in *Mountaineering—Freedom of the Hills.*

Let's look at some of the situations we may run into in the wilderness. For the purpose of this book, we are not mountain climbers, much less rock climbers. We are backpackers and mountaineers. We will be travelling almost entirely on trails, some maintained and patrolled more than others. We will rarely hike cross-country, and then not where there are such conditions that we would need a rope or other safety equipment.

We can still fall and hurt ourselves, but the injury will usually be minor. One hazard is that, particularly during the first days of a backpack trip, we are not accustomed to having 30 to 50 pounds strapped to our back. Our center of gravity is radically shifted. A sideways lunge, from which we would quickly recover under normal circumstances, can be unstoppable. With your feet out from under you, you are just another bit of matter insofar as gravity is concerned, and you start accelerating downwards, covering 16 feet that first second. It's all over very quickly. So don't fall, most particularly into a stream or river, swollen and fast-moving with early summer snowmelt. When crossing such a stream, use extreme caution, and have your backpack unbuckled, ready to slip out of instantly if you should be swept off your feet.

After the fall I mentioned earlier, when the weight of my pack and of my arrogance threw me off balance, I decided that it would be a splendid idea to spend a couple of minutes before each backpack trip getting used to the effects of this additional weight. I reasoned that it would be of benefit to stand with my backpack on, making little lunges and false slips, sensing how the pack's weight would affect my response. I still think it's a splendid idea, but I've never gotten around to trying it.

Can you get sick in the mountains—sick in the normal sense of the word as the flat-landers use it? Sure, but you are more apt to have brought the illness with you. If you have a bad cold or some other debilitating sickness, don't go backpacking. Your body has enough to do already, fighting the infection. You'll just make yourself and everyone else miserable. There isn't as much chance of the fresh air making you feel better as there is of the exercise and thin air making you feel worse. You'll be a pain to everyone with your sneezing and moaning.

The chances that you will contract any kind of sickness in the mountains is rather remote. People spread most of the harmful bacteria, and there just aren't many people where you're going. Those who are there are in much better health, all in all, than those who aren't there. Therefore, there aren't as many germs around to get into your system, unless you bring some with you, or play with rabid ground squirrels, or have some amazingly unsanitary habits.

Vitamin pills? Sure. If you take them at home, you might as well bring them along. You'll probably be eating more healthful food than you do at home, since carrying chocolate cream pies, pork chops, and French fried potatoes in your pack is rather impractical. Even if you had to live on white rice for a week in the mountains, you're not going to come down with beriberi or pellagra. Your mountain diet might bore you senseless, but it won't hurt you physically in a week or so. I take a multi-vitamin tablet every day on a backpack, if I remember to do so, just as I do at home. I doubt that I derive much benefit from it, but it's a habit.

If your body overheats on the trail, try splashing cold water on the back of your neck. If that doesn't shape you up in a hurry, submerge your wrists in a stream or lake, then add your bare feet if you want to go whole hog.

The other way around, if you start to feel chilly on the trail, remember that you lose body heat the fastest from your head and from your mid-section. Put on a hat or cap, pull a wool cap down over your ears, and wrap a wool scarf around your waist under your shirt. The heat you save will be your own, and will warm the rest of you.

If you start getting light-headed on the trail and you have done nothing to deliberately induce this condition, you may be having a touch of altitude sickness. This is due to insufficient oxygen reaching the brain, and the symptoms and treatment are about the same as for shock. Lie down, keep warm, raise your feet higher than your head. Try this for ten minutes, and if you're not back to normal, or at least acceptably close to normal, you'd best head back down the mountain for a day in the denser air.

Always try to arrive at your trailhead the afternoon or evening before the backpack starts. Spending a night at the trailhead's elevation will make the next day much easier, much more comfortable. It will lessen the possibility of altitude sickness or at least its severity and duration. Altitude sickness in its milder forms is quite common. Symptoms can include fatigue, headache, loss of appetite, nausea, vomiting, shortness of breath, and difficulty in sleeping for a night or two.

With rest and nourishment, you'll usually feel better the next morning. If not, it's better to head down the trail to the roadhead, even on into a motel in town. Otherwise you'll have a horrible outing, plus being a bore to your companions.

With slower ascents as backpackers, as contrasted to the gung-ho peak baggers, you will be less apt to have trouble with altitude sickness, but it can happen. Even less of a worry, but one of which you should be aware, is high altitude pulmonary edema. The cause is basically the same as with altitude sickness: a lack of sufficient oxygen. But here the end effect is a congestion—or too much blood—in the lungs, brain, and other vital organs. The early symptoms are the same as for altitude sickness, but there is greater restlessness, coughing, and finally frothy, bloody sputum hacked up from the lungs. With these symptoms, particularly the bloody coughings, you must get the

*There are few germs in the cold, clear mountain air. This is the 13,777-foot Trail Crest pass near Mt. Whitney.*

victim down the mountain immediately, at least 2,000 feet of elevation down, and preferably to a hospital and medical attention. Use a continuous supply of oxygen, if at all possible.

As I mentioned, this is a rare affliction, even among mountain climbers in the high country of the Himalayas, but it can happen at much lower elevations. It is one of those possibilities that you should file away in an obscure corner of your mind, never worrying about it, but never forgetting about it.

There is one school of thought on the ill effects of the lowered oxygen supply which believes that much of the trouble is caused by a change in body acidity. For mountain climbers, hurrying upwards more rapidly than we backpackers normally do, this school would have the climber chew an occasional Tums or Rolaid, monitoring his tongue from time to time with litmus paper. Now, you should have Tums or Rolaids in your first aid kit anyway, so the next time anyone in your party has a touch of altitude sickness, give them one and see what happens.

Part of our mountain medicine thinking is based around the Ten Essentials. You will run across this idea in many of the up-to-date books on backpacking and mountaineering. The list of essentials may vary slightly in content and in the number of items, but the point is always to have with you those things which you cannot do without, and cannot improvise, in a real emergency.

Here are the "Ten Essentials" as listed by the Mountaineering Training Course given by the Angeles Chapter of the Sierra Club:

To find your way

1. Map of the area
2. Compass
3. Flashlight

For your protection

4. Sunglasses
5. Extra food and water
6. Extra clothing

For emergencies

7. Waterproof matches
8. Candle or fuel tablets
9. Pocket knife
10. First aid kit

All this, in a nylon bag, should weigh no more than two pounds. Each person on any backpack, hike, or climb should have his or her own set of the Ten Essentials. The very idea of them is that they will add to your comfort and may save your life in an emergency situation. That emergency could well be that you are separated from the other members of your party, and/or that you have to spend the night away from your main backpack and equipment. And, you may be injured.

I try to carry at least two maps of the wilderness area that I'm travelling in: a U.S. Geological Survey topographical map which is highly detailed, and a forest service or park service map, which is more up-to-date. Many of the topos of the Sierra Nevada, for instance, have not been updated or resurveyed in 20 years or more. If you suddenly need an escape route on a long backpack, you most certainly don't want to head up some canyon blindly, hoping that there is a reasonably easy route out of the wilderness. You *must* know that your escape route is feasible, and you can only determine this from your maps. It is also nice to have the adjoining topos to the ones actually needed for your route, so that you can identify peaks and valleys off in the distance.

The best type of compass is the "orienteering" kind, such as the Silva, sold by most of the equipment suppliers. This type can be used for low-order plane table surveying for accurately fixing your position on the topo map, as well as for following a predetermined compass course. There are several good booklets out on map and compass work, and the Boy Scout *Fieldbook* has a section on it.

The flashlight that you carry in your Ten Essentials should be strictly for emergency use. You may need eight hours of light from it, if you should have to come out at night. If the flashlight is such that you can easily open and close it, reverse one of the batteries so that it cannot be accidentally turned on in your pack. If you try this with one of the little Mallory flashlights, you will end up with bits and pieces all over the ground. The best answer to this is to tape the switch closed.

You should carry extra batteries, which I usually do, and an extra bulb, which I usually don't. With the little three-ounce Mallory it is much simpler to carry a complete extra flashlight.

Incidentally, in the January 1979 *American Rifleman* magazine, a letter to the editor brings up a danger in the practice of reversing one cell in a flashlight. The writer states that if this is done with Nicad (nickel cadmium) rechargeable cells, the flashlight could explode. He goes on to say that this is a common warning given by the Nicad battery manufacturers, but not by flashlight manufacturers.

I wear prescription sunglasses most of the time on the trail, even at lower elevations. Higher, the sunlight can be quite intense, particularly when bouncing off snow or light-colored rocks. In my Ten Essentials bag I also have a pair of lightweight, folding snow goggles as used by mountain climbers. You'll find them in most of the suppliers' catalogs, although the old $1.00 a pair Everest goggles seem to be gone. Carry a spare pair, in case your regular dark glasses get broken or glissade in between the rocks of a boulder field.

Extra food will not be a lifesaver, in all probability, but it certainly could make you more comfortable if you have to spend the night in the boonies without some of your other camping gear. I carry a small can of government surplus pemmican. This glop was worked out by government nutritionists, and has no connection whatsoever with Arctic pemmican. It is really a high-energy fruitcake and isn't too bad tasting, particularly if you pour a little rum into it a half-hour before eating. You could also carry a small can of Spam or corned beef, making certain that you have some way to open the can.

You should have an extra quart of water with you at all times. Some backpackers carry several smaller plastic water bottles to minimize the risk of having one leak out all its contents. I refill my water bottle at every opportunity as the water sources shown on the maps may be dry or polluted. I screw the cap back on tightly after each drink; never set down an open water bottle or canteen. An accidental spill could be very inconvenient!

As backpackers, we have the Ten Essentials and more with us in our backpack. The reason for concentrating the ten in one small bag is so that you can leave your main pack, and with a light day pack, make a short afternoon hike in safety. Never be without your Ten Essentials!

I usually have all my extra clothes in my backback, but if I'm going off on a side trip away from my main pack, I'll sort through them carefully. Even under fairly warm conditions I'll include a sweater, windproof parka, long pants (if I'm wearing shorts during the day), and wool gloves. The point is not only to be ready for sudden weather changes during the day, but to be ready in case I should have to spend a night out in the open. The other extra clothes I carry in my Ten Essentials bag is a space blanket—one of those tightly folded, two-ounce sheets of thin mylar, with an aluminized coating. This would be my sleeping bag in an emergency.

The waterproof match container I carry is a plastic creation that I have only seen in the L. L. Bean catalog, although I'm sure they must be available elsewhere. It has a small compass on one end and a police whistle on the other. In with the matches I have a small strip of sandpaper, about a quarter-inch by an inch. Trying to strike wooden matches when everything around you is wet or frozen can be quite a chore, if not impossible. I also carry several boxes of waterproof and/or windproof matches in different parts of my backpack, along with the paper matches in their Ziploc bags.

Although I have never had to use it, some kind of fire starter could prove quite essential. I carried fuel tabs for awhile, but found that they lost much of their flammability with time, which made them rather useless. I now carry a plastic vial with four short sections of candle. Each is cut about two inches in

*With shelter up, and water supply assured, author is set for the night. Flower Lake, above Onion Valley.*

length, with the wax stripped off for an inch, to provide a long and easily lit wick.

I always carry a fairly heavy pocket knife in my pants pocket plus a thin and light Swiss Army Cadet model in the Ten Essentials bag. All the blades are kept sharp—the resharpening being one of the first tasks on the return home after each trip. A dull knife is useless, if not necessarily pointless.

Almost every book on backpacking and mountaineering contains a long list of things that should be in your outdoor first aid kit. This book will be no exception. Most of the first aid kits sold by suppliers are both inadequate and heavy. Put together your own, fitting, it into a plastic refrigerator box if you can.

### Backpacker's first aid kit

Triangular bandage: for arm sling

Ace elastic bandage: for sprains

Large gauze dressing: for large wounds

Three 3x3 gauze dressings: for small wounds

Roll of one-inch adhesive tape

Band Aids

Moleskin: for blisters

Popsicle sticks: for finger splints

Small bar of soap: for cleaning wounds

Aspirin or Tylenol: for mild pain, headaches

Chapstick or similar lip ointment

Tums or Rolaids: for acidity

Ex-Lax: for constipation

Lomotil prescription: for diarrhea

Empirin with codeine (prescription): moderate pain, headache

Tweezer and needles: for splinters, blisters

Folding scissors

Safety pins

Throat lozenges

Vaseline

Water purification tablets

Cutter snakebite kit

Add anything else that you feel is important. Tape two dimes to the bottom of the lid, so you can reach the operator from an isolated pay phone in the outback. This emergency service that should be free isn't yet.

Remember that three of anything is a widely recognized call of distress—shouts, whistles, blasts, fires, flashlight flashes. If you have to use such a distress call, just hope that whoever sees or hears it recognizes it for what it is. Would you?

# 13

# Mountain Weather

Mountain weather has several unusual features which we are not apt to encounter elsewhere. The first is that we are there, in the high mountains, or we wouldn't be worrying about it in the first place. Nearer to sea level, if not nearer to God, we are at the bottom of a vast ocean of air. When we are several miles up a mountain, we are on an island in the sky. At 18,000 feet, half of the air would be below us. Thus, islands and archipelagos break up the more or less smooth currents of the air-ocean and often create their own local weather, or "microclimates," if you will.

Another possible difficulty with mountain weather lies in the fact that most of our backpacking travel follows trails in the valleys, between the high peaks and ridges. We can't see the sky near the horizon, so can't see a storm on its way.

It is this sudden and unexpected storm that is the threat. We usually have a pretty good idea of the normal weather patterns for the area where we are backpacking, or certainly should. In some, as in the Sierra Nevada of California, the vast majority of the weather moves in from the west or northwest. There, if you see no clouds by noon, you can figure on being safe in the evening, other than the harmless "Sierra Crest clouds." These form in good weather as the gradually rising air from the west drops over the steep eastern escarpment. In the Rocky Mountains, I have been told, you can bank on afternoon thunderstorms during the summer, so you should try to get all your climbing and hiking done early in the day. This is the sort of weather on which you can plan.

What you have to watch out for is any change in the weather, any change in the wind direction, and change in the mood of the place. My son and I were camped at Flower Lake, west of Onion Valley in the Sierra, several summers ago. We were on our way out from a week's backpack. We were a day ahead of our schedule, so planned to spend two nights at this beautiful lake. The first morning, though, as we were preparing to move our camp a few hundred yards to an even jazzier spot I had located, we noticed the clouds moving in over the top of the nearby ridge. At eight in the morning, fast, and from the south. Everything was wrong. We loaded up our packs quickly and headed down the trail, getting to the van with the rain hitting just behind us, and lightning crashing off of the peaks.

It was one of those unexpected moist air masses that sweep up from Mexico and the Pacific. There probably had been a few days warning, but it had come long after we had headed in a week before.

What can you do if you are far back in the mountains when such a storm comes your way? Well, this is what the planning and preparedness that we wrote about in earlier chapters is all about! This is why you carry the Ten Essentials, and why you have certain clothes and equipment with you, even in the summer. If, as in many parts of the Sierra, the only escape route is over a 13,000-foot "mountaineer's pass," you're going to have to sit out the storm. If you have the necessary equipment, this means only a little inconvenience, perhaps a little sogginess, and a helluva story to tell when you get back.

Last summer, in 1978, tropical storm *Norma* swept up the Sierra Nevada out of Mexico in early September. It lasted three or four days with rain and snow. Two groups of two people died from exposure, or "hypothermia," as we call it now. Others in the Sierra at the same time saw the storm approaching, set up camp, and got ready for the worst. Inside a tent, in dry clothes, and inside a dry sleeping bag, things may have gotten a little boring. But it sure beats being dead.

As reported in the September 8, 1978 *Los Angeles Times*, two of the four hikers were a father and son, aged 66 and 35. Wearing nothing but cut-off jeans, T-shirts, and hiking boots, the hikers were caught by the storm at 11,000 feet on Mt. Whitney. An Inyo County sheriff's spokesman said that they had a tent with them, but apparently had not tried to use it. One man was found dead in his soggy sleeping bag.

The other two, a young man and woman, were reported to have been slightly more warmly dressed, but were definitely not carrying bad weather gear.

From this bare-boned newspaper report, I think you can see where these four people were wrong, wrong, wrong. Mountain weather is something to try to understand, to be prepared for, but not to fear. Like the other parts of nature, the weather isn't out to harm you, nor to help you. It just is. It's up to you to use the weather, to live within it, and to watch out for the phases of it that could be harmful to your health. The weather is as much a part of the awesomeness of the mountains as are the rocks and the trees.

If you are high on a peak, or are crossing a pass, and you see a storm coming, of course you should immediately head for lower ground. If you had real expedition equipment, you could survive high winds and low temperatures. We will assume,

| Wind Speed M.P.H. | Chill Factor Temperatures in Degrees Fahrenheit | | | | | | | | |
|---|---|---|---|---|---|---|---|---|---|
| 0 | 40 | 35 | 30 | 25 | 20 | 20 | 15 | 5 | 0 |
| 5 | 35 | 30 | 25 | 20 | 15 | 10 | 5 | 0 | -5 |
| 10 | 30 | 20 | 15 | 10 | 5 | 0 | -10 | -15 | -20 |
| 15 | 25 | 15 | 10 | 0 | -5 | -10 | -20 | -25 | -30 |
| 20 | 20 | 10 | 5 | 0 | -10 | -15 | -25 | -30 | -35 |
| 25 | 15 | 10 | 0 | -5 | -10 | -20 | -30 | -35 | -45 |
| 30 | 10 | 5 | 0 | -10 | -20 | -25 | -35 | -40 | -50 |
| 35 | 10 | 5 | -5 | -10 | -20 | -30 | -35 | -40 | -50 |
| 40 | 10 | 0 | -5 | -15 | -20 | -30 | -35 | -45 | -55 |

Adapted from Military Windchill Chart in "Hypothermia: Killer of the Unprepared," by the author.

though, that you're not carrying gear suitable for Everest or K2. Your job is to look for natural protection from the storm. There may not be too much that you can do about rain and hail coming straight down, but you can get out of the wind. It's that wind that is the biggest threat!

One thing that you should understand, although not necessarily remember the numerical details of, is the wind chill factor. This is what will knock you off; this is what is usually behind deaths from exposure or hypothermia. What the chart shows is that the actual, physical temperature of the air is only a part of the problem of staying warm. If there is a wind, and there almost always is in the mountains, its effect on the human body is to lower its temperature more than the air's actual temperature would itself. If the air temperature is 40 degrees, but you are standing in a 30 mile an hour wind, your skin will not be at 40 degrees, but at 10 degrees. Normally the only precaution you would have to take would be putting on a windproof jacket and a sweater. This wind chill factor is not a threat in itself.

The danger is greatest when you are caught out in a storm, tired, and your clothes become wet. Now the air blowing across your body is in almost direct contact with your skin, with no insulating layer to keep in your body's warmth, and with the additional cooling effect of evaporating water. The heat of your body—the only supply you have with you—quickly disappears downwind. If you don't get out of that wind, fast, and conserve some of your body's heat, the heat loss goes deeper and deeper into your body's interior. The equipment in there begins to malfunction, and there is a rapid and progressive mental and physical collapse. This is what happened to the four people who died in the Sierra last summer. They needn't have done so.

Once your body's inner temperature drops below about 95 degrees Fahrenheit, its heat is lost faster than it can be replaced by normal body activity. The first signs of this heat loss are shivering and trying to build up body heat by exercising. With continued heat loss, the victim soon becomes exhausted and disoriented. His judgment and reasoning are affected, and he may make no attempts to prevent advancing collapse and death which can take place in a matter of a few hours.

Doesn't that sound like the father and son in the newspaper

*Rain and snow erode the mountains, and trails must be maintained and rebuilt.*

report, never attempting to use their tent, the one piece of equipment which might have saved their lives?

The basic enemy is not the cold as such, but the wind and the wetness, so be prepared with waterproof and windproof clothes. Wool, or the new Holofil II and PolarGuard synthetics, are the only materials that will insulate you when wet. The three factors beyond the wind and the wet which can vastly increase the possibilities of hypothermia are: poor physical condition, exhaustion, and lack of heat-producing food to help keep up your body's production of heat.

Therefore, don't backpack when already tired. Do hole up before you become exhausted. Get out of the wind and the wet, and munch on a candy bar or other quick-energy foods.

I cannot stress too highly that planning, preparation, and knowing when to turn back—or wariness, to match my earlier explanation—are everything!

You can get trapped by hypothermia without realizing it. Solo backpacking or mountaineering can be dangerous due to this hazard alone. Keep an eye on other people—watch anyone who gets unusually drowsy, who shivers, who stumbles frequently, or who hallucinates. Take that person out of the wind and wetness right away, right now! Get them dry and into a dry sleeping bag. Give them warm, even hot, drinks; you must get their body core warmed up. Transferring body heat in a sleeping bag by skin-to-skin contact is a very effective method of treatment, and certainly makes for a "shared experience." Don't let the victim go to sleep until his body temperature is nearly normal; sleep at this point is quite likely to be fatal.

With adequate equipment, and a proper attitude, a touch of "bad weather" can add a lot of fun and games to a backpacking trip: lightning bolts snapping at the higher peaks, rain on the tent roof, snow flakes floating out of an afternoon sky, a fog that thins ahead of you as you climb a morning pass, thunder muttering in a distant canyon.

Too much bad weather can be a pain, but a little can be a fascinating change of pace.

# 14

# Because They're There

It was George Leigh-Mallory, back in the 1920s, who said that the reason he and his party were going to try to climb Mt. Everest was "Because it's there." This is much of the reason we backpackers go to the mountains today. Some will claim that this is an "escape from reality." I have never been able to comprehend why the man-made cities are "reality," and the natural world out there is "unreality."

It is similar to the conservationist's belief that we must give way for an "endangered species" of falcon or pup fish, without considering that *we* may also be one of the endangered species. The cities are natural and are reality, too, in that they are a product of Man, who is one of the animals on the face of the earth.

No matter what your logic, a city must be accepted as being as "natural" as a termite mound or a prairie dog village. If, then, both the cities and the wilderness are natural, and are reality, we escape from nothing by going to the other. What we may do is to escape from one condition of reality, by spending time in another, and thus gain more appreciation and understanding of both.

Now, most of our backpacking will be done in the mountains. The reason is obvious. There is more variety of nature, of reality, in the mountains than on the flat ground. No matter how charming the natives and the countryside, a week's backpack across Kansas would not be a sparkling and memorable experience.

With the development of Alfred Wegener's continental drift theories into the more solidly-based plate tectonics theory of today, we are beginning to understand much more about how many of the earth's mountain chains formed.

If we avoid the question of the underlying forces (literally and figuratively) which cause the giant plates to move and thereby form the mountains, we can still say that all mountains have one of three not always distinct origins.

Many very high mountains are volcanic. This ties in nicely with plate tectonics, with one plate sliding under another, or *subducting*. The Cascades are a fine example, as is Orizaba, the highest peak in Mexico, and Aconcagua, the highest peak in the Western Hemisphere.

Other mountain ranges are caused by faulting and the uptilting of huge masses of rock. The California Sierra Nevada is a textbook example. The fault is on the east, the hingepoint on the west. The western slope is gradual, the eastern sheer.

A more common origin of mountains is by stupendous lateral forces, pushing horizontally rather than more vertically as with fault block mountains. When huge areas of land are pushed together—and the forces which cause this pushing are not yet understood—the all-too-solid rock can assume plastic qualities and can bend and twist to amazing degrees.

Sometimes the limits of elasticity are reached, the thick sections of strained rock tear apart, and one section of rock overrides another. To a geologist, this overriding can be quite obvious; there is a repetition of beds and formations. Geological history seems to be repeating itself. In the case of the underside of a looping fold doing the overriding, you could and do have a particular sequence of rock beds at the bottom, a reversed sequence above that, then a normal sequence again above that.

This forward in time, backward in time, forward in time pattern of rock formations does occur, and it is why we do know a great deal about why mountains form, even if we don't yet know the power source behind the movement.

As backpackers rather than geologists, we can enjoy the consequences of these mountain-building forces without trying to understand all the whys and wherefores. Mountain masses have

*Giant forces have created the world's mountain ranges. Here we are near the high point of the uptilted Sierra Nevada fault block, on 13,632-foot University Peak, looking west down the block's slope.*

been pushed up for miles from the surrounding surface, tens of miles. Similarly unbelievable masses of rock have been eroded away, ever so slowly, by wind, rain, and glaciation.

The valleys are often filled with debris washed from the

mountains to the depth of miles, tens of miles again, sinking slowly as the load accumulates. All of this takes millions of years and we are seeing a single, almost-static instant in geological time. But, by travelling to different mountains, or even different parts of the same mountains, we can catch this geological history at different points in time.

One of the mineral specimens in my office is a chunk of anorthosite, from the San Gabriel Mountains directly north of Los Angeles. It is accurately dated as having solidifed and crystallized 1,200,000,000 years ago. It helps to keep me in my place as an extremely recent, and probably very temporary, inhabitant of this planet Earth.

Mineral collecting, more popularly called "rockhounding," is a little outside the subject of backpacking, if only because of the weight problem. If you must gather mineral specimens, try to do so on the way out, when your pack is lighter, and the distances shorter. And remember that you are not allowed to take mineral, animal, or vegetable material from national parks or wilderness areas—plus some national monuments.

*U-shaped valleys are a good indication of glacial erosion, which was heavy in parts of the Sierra Nevada of California.*

*Sometimes you need four-wheel drive to get to a remote and unmaintained roadhead.*

Rockhounding and mineralogy cannot be covered in the short space that I have here, so I would call your attention to my book, *The Young Rockhound's Handbook*, which is listed in more detail in chapter 17. As is brought out in this book, mineral identification seems complicated and confusing at first, but is really not all that difficult in reality. While it is true that there are more than 2,500 recognized mineral species, the vast majority of these are quite rare. If you get so that you can recognize 50 or 60, you can identify almost any rock or mineral that you find in the field.

*A $25 coated nylon tent, laundry drying behind*

The best place to see the basic minerals and the typical rocks of any area is in the collections of local museums, rock shops, and Chambers of Commerce. Even with practice, you won't be able to identify everything you find, but neither can most graduate mineralogists—not in the field. But you will be able to identify the majority of the rocks and minerals that you see and make a pretty good guess at the others. Your companions will be quite impressed. Or bored.

The same goes for identifying plants, animals, and insects. There are many field guides on the market and they are usually regional, as they should be. Check your local library and bookstore. Even a quick study of any of them may well increase the pleasure of your next backpack trip. I have never really understood why being able to name a thing makes it more enjoyable, but this seems to be so. I once knew the difference between a Jeffrey and a Ponderosa pine, and I should relearn it.

Perhaps I will. Next season.

# 15

# Mountain Photography

Memories should be locked inside your head. I shudder a little mentally each time I see a hiker or backpacker whip out his camera to photograph a striking scene, rather than standing there and recording it in his brain. I usually criticize the way he is taking the photograph—silently, of course—but that isn't the point. Memories are unexplainable souvenirs lodged in your mind, not little scraps of paper. The photo prints will become lost, will be thrown out with the fish wrapper. The deeply-impressed memories within your head will last you the rest of your life. They may even *be* the rest of your life.

I always carry my camera deep inside my backpack, and never take it out unless I have a definite need for a particular photo, such as for a magazine article, or for this book. I have carried my Pentax on week-long backpack trips and shot two photos. I have carried it on another and shot 300. But I was not shooting these so that I could remember what the countryside looked like. I know that; that's stored away in the complexity of my neurons and synapses. I took the photos to show other people what the countryside looked like or what a tent was.

The majority of people today shoot color film. I almost never do. The reason is the same as before: I shoot photos for illustrations, and very few of my markets are interested in color photography. Therefore, I shoot black and white in the Pentax. If I need color, I take along my old Minolta Autocord 2¼ x 2¼

*Mt. Whitney Trail, Inyo National Forest*

*The mountains of Tennessee have enough haze to soften the distance background right out of existance. Filters could counteract some of this. (Tennessee Department of Tourist Development)*

*It is important to get at least one person in the foreground of each photo to give scale and human interest. Cirque Peak at left.*

twin-lens reflex for that specific purpose. I haven't done so in half a dozen years.

My point is this—before you carry a heavy camera and other photo equipment on a backpacking trip, ask yourself if you really and truly want any photos of the trip. So many people that I see take snapshots rather than photographs anyhow— they whip up their Instamatic or Polaroid camera at every view-point without even thinking of what it is that they are trying to capture on film. Nature is art, quite true, but it isn't artistically arranged from every angle.

The painter can rearrange the elements of a given scene to create a better balance. The photographer is forced to move himself and his camera to achieve the same thing. If you want to photograph a particular scene—say, the view from a high mountain pass—study the scene from the standpoint of how it will look on hard, cold photographic paper. Perhaps moving a few feet up the hillside will add something of interest in the foreground, something to give depth to an otherwise flat and static scene. Whenever possible, have some people in the fore-ground. They add both a sense of depth and of humanity.

Nothing is more ghastly and amateurish in a photograph than a group of people all leering into the camera lens and out at the viewer. Few people stand around the real world and gri-mace at each other. Let the people in your photograph be looking off at a distant peak or eating their lunches. If they're friends or relations, you'll be able to recognize them on the print even though they aren't gawking out at you. If they are strangers, who gives a damn what their faces looked like any-way. But do try to get at least one person into every outdoors photo.

I am in several of the photos in this book only because there was no one else around at the time. That sounds a little puz-zling, but it is one of the prices I pay for solo hiking and solo backpacking. The answer to photographing the lonely solo backpacker is the self-timer built into many modern cameras. The Minolta Autocord has one, as does the Pentax. My son's older model Pentax does not. You can buy a separate self-timer, which fits on the end of a cable release, at most photo stores.

Plan your photo scene with an invisible person somewhere in the foreground. Then balance the camera on a rock or a post to cover the intended scene, push the self-timer button, and become visible. Most self-timers will give you about 15 seconds before tripping the camera's shutter. Depending on the distance to the spot you have chosen, walk quickly or run like the devil, trying to get there and into a relaxed pose before the shutter opens. It is a good idea to try two or three shots, as there is no way of knowing exactly how the camera caught you. In the stillness of the outdoors, you usually hear the shutter go off, but then it's too late to alter your pose.

One way to beat the problem of finding a flat rock or a post at the location where you want to shoot your photos with the self-timer is to carry a tripod. Most are too large and too heavy, although I recently ordered one by mail that weighs exactly a pound and sells for $19.95. This was from Porter's Camera Store, Inc., Box 628, Cedar Falls, Iowa 50613. Write for their free catalog.

Another possibility is to buy a camera support clamp, which has an adjustable head that screws into the threaded hole on the bottom of most cameras. The clamp itself can be tightened around an ice axe head, a cane handle, or a small-diameter limb. There is also an auger, which can be screwed into a tree or a log. Several of the backpacker supply catalogs list these for about $10. I carried one for years, used it twice, and now leave it at home. Every once in awhile I come upon a photographic situation where it would be extremely handy and wish I had it with me.

As an outdoors photographer, you will soon discover that there is nothing duller than a crystal-clear sky. Everyone else is as happy as a bear with the horizon-to-horizon blueness. Photographically, however, the sky is empty, empty. You pray for just one or two lousy little cumulus clouds to break up the drab monotony of the sky.

Can we defeat a perfect day for the sake of our art? Well, yes, a little. To darken the sky slightly for black and white photography, to contrast it more with the light-colored rocks, we can use a filter in front of the lens. In the mountains I always keep a 2X yellow filter on the Pentax. It darkens the sky a little and makes clouds stand out more sharply. A 2X red filter would darken the sky and heighten the contrast even more, with a 4X red giving a slightly unrealistic look. The 2X and 4X tell you the filter factor, which means you must increase the exposure that much to compensate for the loss of light through the colored filter. Photos taken using these lenses are dramatic, definitely dramatic.

In shooting color at higher elevations, Eastman recommends a UV filter. This is a clear disk which filters out some of the ultraviolet light, which is more intense where the air is thinner, and will otherwise give a strange purplish sky.

Although I have been a professional photographer during most of my adult life, I do not try to eyeball exposure settings, particularly in the mountains. The light is intense and the circumstances unfamiliar. My eyes adapt to the brightness without notifying my brain of the fact, and I'm apt to overexpose anything I guess at. So I carry an exposure meter. Now, I may only take a reading every hour or so, but I need to know the basic exposure for the particular place and time of day.

Modern black and white film is quite forgiving insofar as overexposure or underexposure go. You can be a stop or two off in either direction, and still end up with printable negatives. Not so with color film. When I shoot color, I meter every shot.

In using a meter, the strongest reading will be from the brightest part of the scene, which may not be the part of the scene that you want to be right on. Thus, particularly for color, I take a series of readings: the sky, the rock, the trees, the palm of my hand (for skin tones), and perhaps a reading on the sun as the source light. Then I set my exposure based on what part of the light intensity range I want to be the most true.

In shooting many thousands of photographs, I have found that f/11 is the best all-around diaphragm stop with the present-day Japanese lenses. Unless there is some pressing reason for doing otherwise, I leave the diaphragm set at f/11 and adjust my exposure with the shutter speed. As there is very little fast action involved in most of my photography, I can use anything between 1/30 and 1/500 of a second. This gives me the equivalent of a four f/stop range, keeping the fine depth of field sharpness that f/11 produces. The majority of the photographs in this book were taken that way, using Eastman Plus-X or Panatomic-X film.

One difficulty in mountain photography is the very clearness

*Solid rock is folded and tilted by internal pressures. This is a road cut through the San Andreas fault zone near Palmdale, California.*

of the air. Unless you specifically look for it, you don't notice how much the thicker and dirtier air nearer sea level softens the background in photos. This makes a pleasing effect, with the main subject of the photo crisp and sharp, the distant hills

*Rain clouds move in from the west in the high Sierra Nevada country.*

*Clearness of the air at 14,000 feet makes this photo of Mt. Whitney too sharp with little sense of depth due to normal softening.*

slightly softened. But at higher elevations you lose most or all of that softening and are apt to forget it until you have your prints made. There is your subject in the foreground, razor-sharp, with the mountains ten miles away also razor-sharp. Every damn thing in the photograph is razor-sharp, and the photograph is confusing. The photograph is "busy." You can't separate the men from the mountains. Rats!

I have come up with only one solution to this problem. Throw the distant background slightly out of focus deliberately. If you are using a fast film, such as Tri-X, this can present a problem, as you have no room left to play around with maintaining the correct exposure while cross-adjusting the diaphragm and shutter speeds. You're already at f/11 at 1/500, and there's nowhere to go. In this situation, with the lens giving very good depth of field at f/11, about all you can do is to bring that depth of field in very close. If the subject of the photo—the person, that is—is standing 15 feet away, try focusing at five feet. What you're trying to do is to let the lens' depth of field carry out to the person and perhaps slightly beyond, but not to the infinity of the background. Here, I'd try several shots, with the lens' distance set at, say, ten, seven, five, and three feet. One of these shots will fuzz the background ever so slightly.

With a slower film, where you might normally be set at f/11 at 1/125 of a second, you can open up the lens' diaphragm to reduce the depth of field while speeding up the shutter speed to compensate for the increase in total light to the film. Many modern cameras have the shutter speeds marked so that they are the equivalents of f/stops. Thus the difference between one f/stop on the stop adjusting collar matches those on the shutter speed adjusting collar. One stop wider open for the lens, one shutter speed stop faster for the shutter.

There are many excellent books out on photography, if you feel that you need to read about it. The important question, insofar as this book is concerned, is do you really need any photographs of your trip and, if so, how many? Aren't your memories enough to last you a lifetime?

There is a woodsy saying, sponsored by Eastman Kodak: "Take only photographs, leave only footprints." Maybe we should take nothing, and leave nothing. Maybe we should take only memories, and leave only fading ghosts of our passing.

# 16

# Winter Backpacking

*U.S. News & World Report* for January 15, 1979, listed some figures from the U.S. Department of the Interior estimating the number of people in this country, over the age of 12, who participate at least five times a year in various sports and recreations. Among these were 28.1 million for "Hiking and Backpacking," 15.0 million for "Primitive-site Camping," and 2.0 million for "Cross-country Skiing."

Even with a lot of nit-picking as to how the Department of the Interior defined "hiking and backpacking"—they never contacted me, so I don't know—there are obviously still an awful lot of people out on the wilderness trails in the United States every summer.

How can we beat the overcrowding? How can we get away from wall-to-wall backpackers? One solution is to avoid the better-known and heavily-used trails and areas. The other is to do as much of your backpacking as you can during the off-season. If any area will be crowded at all, it will be most so between Memorial Day and Labor Day.

To carry this last solution to overcrowding to its ultimate, the least-crowded time of the year will be in the middle of winter. There's no one out there; even the bears are hibernating. So why don't more people backpack in the winter? Because they don't realize that it's possible, that's why!

Now, I've talked elsewhere in this book about how crucial it is to have adequate survival equipment with you always, and how you should be prepared for the worst weather, even in the summer. In early summer you may have to cross snow-blocked passes. In late summer you may have rain, hail, and snow.

What's so different about winter? The difference is mostly one of degree. In the winter it's colder, there is ice and snow on the ground, and there is more likelihood of storms. If you are prepared for these conditions, none of them are that big a deal.

We have talked about insulated clothing. For a winter trip in the mountains you will need more insulation than during any other season. That makes sense.

You can also expect snow and ice on the ground. This can make it a great deal easier to climb a pass or a peak, smoothing over the jagged rock slopes of summer if you have special equipment. This equipment is readily available and is listed in most of the catalogs.

Winter storms can be a problem but, as I said in the chapter on mountain weather, these storms are not "out to get you." They are quite natural, and it's up to you to adapt to them, not they to you. The storms of winter may be more frequent than those of summer, and they may last a little longer. Just as in the summer, you must plan and prepare. You should have your insulated clothes and your shelter. You should carry enough food so that you can stay holed up for three or four days if necessary. You should not panic and try to escape the storm with a frantic dash in the night. You should stay out of the wind, knowing about the wind chill factor and the causes of hypothermia. When a storm is inevitable, lie back and enjoy it.

Since the temperature will be quite a bit lower during any winter backpack trip, you will need clothing and a sleeping bag with more loft, with a thicker layer of insulating airspace, to keep in your body's warmth. Your tent will need to be better-made, stronger, more windproof, more expensive. In most ways winter backpacking is only an extension of spring and fall backpacking, adapted to the more severe conditions.

Even as you should for spring crossings of snow-filled passes, you should have an ice axe and crampons with you in the winter. Crampons strap onto the soles of your boots and give you traction on ice and hard snow where your lug soles would not grip.

*Author and son backpacking on Mt. Shasta*

The ice axe is a walking stick, and a third leg for balance. Having one, you should spend some time practicing "ice axe arrests." If you slip on an icy slope, you roll onto your tightly-held ice axe, angled across your chest, and gently but firmly shove the point of the ice axe's head into the snow or ice. This

*Shawnee State Park, Ohio. (Ohio State Parks)*

131

*Ensolite pads, seen in two of the packs, are used for insulation, not comfort. Kearsarge Pass*

*Plastic tube tents are inexpensive and are weatherproof*

slows and stops your slide. With a little practice it works well and is the only way to stop quickly and safely from a fall on high-angle snow and ice. If you plan to backpack or hike in the mountains in the winter—or anytime there are snow and ice around—you *must* learn how to do an ice axe arrest!

In the usual winter storm which may catch you far back in the wilderness, you may get a foot or more of snow. If you are prepared for a comfortable bivouac, you can wait a day or so after the storm passes to let the snow firm up, then walk out. You may still have to plow through some soft snow and your progress may be slow at times, but with time and survival gear on your side, you will make it out and have quite a story to tell.

The difficulty with soft snow is, obviously, that your feet sink into it. Your weight is spread over the too-small area of your boot soles. There are two mechanical ways to increase the area of your footprint so that you will not sink as deeply into soft snow: snowshoes and skis.

Snowshoes are made of rawhide or plastic webbing stretched across a frame which enlarges the area of your boot by at least ten times and lowers the pounds-per-square-inch loading. While not essential for winter backpacking, a pair of snowshoes could certainly save you many hours of work travelling through soft snow. You can buy snowshoes through some of the dealers listed in chapter 17. Snowshoes have never become an "in" thing in this country, so you'll have to dig a little deeper than usual to find out about them.

In the last few years, cross-country or Nordic skiing has become increasingly popular here. Nordic skiing is different from downhill skiing. The clothes are different, the boots are different, the skis are different, even the people who do Nordic skiing are different! It is closer to snowshoeing than it is to downhill skiing and combines some of both. I list some books on Nordic skiing in chapter 17. It would seem to offer a lot of possibilities for travelling with comparative ease in the snow-bound winter mountains.

However, for the purposes of this book, we are backpackers and we like to walk. Well, you can walk the winter mountains and you can climb the winter peaks. You will need equipment that provides better insulation than you do the rest of the year. You will need an ice axe and some crampons. Your trip might prove more enjoyable if you carried snowshoes or cross-country skis strapped to your pack. You certainly need to build up enough backpacking experience to be able to plan ahead properly, to know how to be prepared, and to know of what to be aware. Start out with easy overnight trips into the edges of the snow country. Read the books listed in chapter 17 on winter camping, hypothermia, avalanches, and frostbite. If at all possible, take a mountaineering course on snow camping.

There's a huge and empty world out there in the winter, just waiting for you!

# 17

# Appendix

Knowing how and where to get information is half the battle. In chapter 2 we listed how to go about getting topographic maps for any part of the United States. In this chapter, I'll give you more sources. First off, a list of books that I have in my backpacking library. They are up-to-date and informative and most likely are the best books available.

Then I'll list backpacking equipment suppliers who I know have free catalogs. These catalogs should be as much a part of your reading as any of the reference books. You can learn much from them, and they are great to dream over.

Next I list the fifty-three chapters of the Sierra Club, and twenty-two of the more active clubs within the Appalachian Trail Conference, by states, alphabetically. Whether you join a club or not is up to you. I definitely recommend your doing so in the beginning. There is no better way to learn your trade.

Next I list some of the better-known commercial tour organizations, as suggested in chapter 11. If you can afford them, they offer some wonderful experiences.

Finally, I will list some odds-and-ends of clubs and organizations in the outdoors and conservation field.

You're at the end of my part of the book. You're finally on your own! In 1780 Edmund Burke said, "Applaud us when we run; console us when we fall; cheer us when we recover; but let us pass on...for God's sake, let us pass on."

I've offered you the freedom of the hills.

Pass on!

## A Backpacker's Library

*Ascent* by Jeremy Bernstein (New York, Random House, 1965).

*Backpack Cookery* by Ruth Dyar Mendenhall (Glendale, La Siesta Press, 1974).

*Backpack Techniques* by Ruth Dyar Mendenhall (Glendale, La Siesta Press, 1973).

*Backpacking* by R.C. Rethmel (Minneapolis, Burgess, 1974).

*Backpacking with Babies and Small Children* by Goldie Silverman (Lynnwood, Signpost, 1975).

*Backpacking: One Step at a Time* by Harvey Manning (Seattle, REI Press, 1972).

*Basic Mountaineering* Henry I. Mandolf, ed. (San Diego, Sierra Club, 1969).

*Basic Rockcraft* by Royal Robbins (Glendale, La Siesta Press, 1971).

*Be an Expert with Map and Compass* by Bjorn Kjellstron (La Porte, American Orienteering Service, 1967).

*The Best About Backpacking* Denise Van Lear, ed. (San Francisco, Sierra Club, 1974).

*Fieldbook* Boy Scouts of America (North Brunswick, 1977).

*Frostbite* by Bradford Washburn (Boston, Museum of Science, 1975).

*How to Live on Nothing* by Joan Ranson Shortney (New York, Pocket Books, 1975).

*How to Survive on Land and Sea* by Frank C. Craighead, Jr. & John J. Craighead (Annapolis, Naval Institute Press, 1977).

*Hypothermia: Killer of the Unprepared* by Theodore G. Lathrop, M.D. (Portland, Mazamas, 1975).

*Knots for Mountaineering* Phil D. Smith (Twentynine Palms, Desert Trails, 1960).

*Medicine for Mountaineering* James A. Wilkerson, M.D., ed. (Seattle, The Mountaineers, 1969).

*Mountaineering: Freedom of the Hills* Peggy Ferber, ed. (Seattle, The Mountaineers, 1977).

*Mountaineering: From Hill Walking to Alpine Climbing* by Alan Blackshaw (Middlesex, Penguin Books, 1968).

*Mountain Operations* U.S. Army Field Manual 31-72 (Washington, D.C., 1959).

*Mountain Rescue Techniques* by Wastl Mariner, Osterreichischer Alpenverein, Innsbruck, Austria (Seattle, The Mountaineers, 1963).

*The New Complete Walker* by Colin Fletcher (New York, Knopf, 1974).

*On Snow and Rock* by Gaston Rebuffat (London, Kay & Ward, 1967).

*Outdoor Living* (Tacoma, Tacoma Mountaineer Rescue Team, no date).

*Outdoor Survival Skills* by Larry Dean Olsen (Provo, Brigham Young University Press, 1973).

*Petersen's Complete Book of Camping & Backpacking* by Thomas F. Patty, photos by W.R.C. Shedenhelm (Los Angeles, Petersen Publishing, 1973).

*The Robin Hood Book* by Bill Kaysing (New York, Link Books, 1974).

*Ropes, Knots & Slings for Climbers* by Walt Wheelock, revised by Royal Robbins (Glendale, La Siesta Press, 1967).

*Scout Handbook* by Frederick L. Hines (North Brunswick, Boy Scouts of America, 1976).

*Snow Avalanche,* Agriculture Handbook No. 194, Forest Service (Washington, D.C., U.S. Dept. of Agriculture, 1961).

*Snow Camping & Mountaineering* by Edward A. Rossit (New York, Funk & Wagnalls, 1974).

*Standard First Aid & Personal Safety* The American National Red Cross (Garden City, Doubleday & Co., 1973).

*True's Hiking and Camping Guide* by W.R.C. Shedenhelm (New York, Fawcett, 1971).

*Vagabonding in America* by Ed Buryn (San Francisco, Ed Buryn, 1976).

*Walking Softly in the Wilderness* by John Hart (San Francisco, Sierra Club, 1977).

*Weather and Weather Forecasting* by A.G. Forsdyke (New York, Bantam Books, 1971).

*Woodcraft & Camping* by Bernard S. Mason (New York, Dover, 1974).

*Young Rockhound's Handbook* by W.R.C. Shedenhelm (New York, Putnam's, 1978).

Here are five publications of which you should be aware if you are planning any winter backpacking or camping. They are all available from World Publications, Inc., 1400 Stierlin Road, Mountain View, California 94043.

*Cross-Country Skiing Guide* by John Hamburger, ed., $3.95.

*Discover Cross-Country Skiing* editors of *Nordic World Magazine,* $1.50.

*Snow Camping* editors of *Nordic World Magazine*, $2.95.

*Training for Nordic Skiing* Dave Prokop, ed., $3.50.

*Winter Safety Handbook* editors of *Nordic World Magazine*, $2.50.

## Equipment Suppliers with Free Catalogs

Adventure 16, Inc.
4620 Alvarado Canyon Rd.
San Diego, Calif. 92120
(714) 283-2374

Camp Trails Company
4111 W. Clarendon Ave.
Phoenix, Ariz. 85019
(602) 272-9401

Co-op Wilderness Supply
1607 Shattuck Ave.
Berkeley, Calif. 94709
(415) 843-9300

Don Gleason's Campers Supply, Inc.
9 Pearl St., P.O. Box 87
Northhampton, Mass. 01060
(413) 584-4895

Early Winters, Ltd.
110 Prefontaine Place So.
Seattle, Wash. 98104
(206) 622-5203

Eastern Mountain Sports, Inc.
6209 Vose Farm Rd.
Peterborough, N.H. 03458
(603) 924-7276

Eddie Bauer
Third & Virginia
Seattle, Wash. 98124
(206) 885-3330

Frostline Kits
Frostline Circle
Denver, Colo. 80241

Holubar Mountaineering, Ltd.
Box 7
Boulder, Colo. 80306
(800) 525-2540 toll-free

JanSport
Paine Field Industrial Park
Everett, Wash. 98204

Kelty
1801 Victory Blvd.
Glendale, Calif. 91201

L.L. Bean, Inc.
3851 Birch St.
Freeport, Me. 04033
(207) 865-3111

Moor & Mountain
63 Park St.
Andover, Mass. 01810
(617) 475-3665

The North Face
P.O. Box 2399, Station A
Berkeley, Calif. 94702
(415) 525-2026

P & S Sales
3818 South 79th East Ave.
Tulsa, Okla. 74145

Recreational Equipment, Inc.
P.O. Box 88125
Seattle, Wash. 98188
(800) 426-4840 toll-free

Rivendell Mountain Works
P.O. Box 199
Victor, Idaho 83455

The Ski Hut
1615 University Ave.
Berkeley, Calif. 94701
(415) 843-8170

Wilderness Experience
20120 Plummer St.
Chatsworth, Calif. 91311

### The Sierra Club

The increasing public interest in the conservation of our planet Earth has skyrocketed the membership of the Sierra Club, founded in 1892 by John Muir. Although still oriented around California and the Sierra Nevada, the club now has fifty-one chapters in the United States and two in Canada.

Most of these chapters in turn have more-localized regional groups, plus committees and sections devoted to everything from Backpacking to Nature Study, from Rock Climbing to Nordic Skiing. You can write to your nearest chapter for further information about its activities. The listing is alphabetically by states.

ALASKA

Alaska Chapter, P.O. Box 2025, Anchorage, Alaska 99510

ARIZONA

Grand Canyon Chapter, 6413 S. 26th St., Phoenix, Ariz. 85040

CALIFORNIA

Kern-Kaweah Chapter, c/o Love, 5805 Daggett Ave., Bakersfield, Calif. 93309
Ventana Chapter, P.O. Box 5667, Carmel, Calif. 93921.
Tehipite Chapter, P.O. Box 5396, Fresno, Calif. 93755
Angeles Chapter, 2410 W. Beverly Blvd., Suite 2, Los Angeles, Calif. 90057
San Francisco Bay Chapter, 6014 College Ave., Oakland, Calif. 94618
Loma Prieta Chapter, 1176 Emerson St., Palo Alto, Calif. 94301

San Gorgonio Chapter, P.O. Box 1023, Riverside, Calif. 92502
Mother Lode Chapter, P.O. Box 1335, Sacramento, Calif. 95806
San Diego Chapter, 1549 El Prado, San Diego, Calif. 92101
Santa Lucia Chapter, Eco Slow, 985 Palm St., San Luis Obispo, Calif. 93401
Los Padres Chapter, P.O. Box 30222, Santa Barbara, Calif. 93105
Redwood Chapter, P.O. Box 466, Santa Rosa, Calif. 95402

COLORADO

Rocky Mountain Chapter, 1325 Delaware, Denver, Colo. 80204

CONNECTICUT

Connecticut Chapter, 60 Washington St., Suite 611, Hartford, Conn. 06106

FLORIDA

Florida Chapter, c/o Coleman, 203 Lake Pansy Dr., Winter Haven, Fla. 33880

GEORGIA

Chattahoochee Chapter, P.O. Box 19574, Station N, Atlanta, Ga. 30325

HAWAII

Hawaii Chapter, P.O. Box 22897, Honolulu, Hawaii 96822

ILLINOIS

Great Lakes Chapter, 53 W. Jackson, Suite 1064, Chicago, Ill. 60604

INDIANA

Hoosier Chapter, P.O. Box 40275, Indianapolis, Ind. 46240

IOWA

Iowa Chapter, P.O. Box 171, Des Moines, Iowa 50301

KANSAS

Kansas Chapter, c/o Jack, 807 Sandusky Ave., Kansas City, Kansas 66101

KENTUCKY

Cumberland Chapter, c/o Criuch, 1362 Bordeaux Dr., Lexington, Ky. 40504

LOUISIANA

Delta Chapter, 111 S. Hennessey St., New Orleans, La. 70119

MARYLAND

Potomac Chapter, c/o Clarke, 402 Burgundy Rd., Rockville, Md. 20850

MASSACHUSETTS

New England Chapter, 3 Joy St., Boston, Mass. 02108

MICHIGAN

Mackinac Chapter, 590 Hollister Bldg., 106 W. Allegan, Lansing, Mich. 48933

MINNESOTA

North Star Chapter, 812 Midland Bank Building, Minneapolis, Minn. 55401

MISSISSIPPI

Mississippi Chapter, P.O. Box 4335, Jackson, Miss. 39216

MISSOURI

Ozark Chapter, P.O. Box 12424, Olivette, Mo. 63132

NEBRASKA

Nebraska Chapter, c/o Warrick, Meadow Grove, Neb. 68752

NEVADA

Toiyabe Chapter, P.O. Box 8096, University Station, Reno, Nev. 89507

NEW JERSEY

New Jersey Chapter, 360 Nassau St., Princeton, N.J. 08540

NEW MEXICO

Rio Grande Chapter, 338 E. DeVargas, Santa Fe, N.M. 87501

NEW YORK
Atlantic Chapter, 800 Second Ave., New York, N.Y. 10017

NORTH CAROLINA

Joseph LeConte Chapter, c/o Lieberman, 7111 Carosan lane, Charlotte, N.C. 28211

OHIO

Ohio Chapter, c/o Rice, 1325 Westminister Dr., Cincinnati, Ohio 45229

OKLAHOMA

Oklahoma Chapter, c/o Wesner, 616 Tulsa, Norman, Okla. 73071

OREGON

Oregon Chapter, c/o Mintkeske, 6815 SE 31st St., Portland, Ore 97202

PENNSYLVANIA

Pennsylvania Chapter, P.O. Box 135, Cogan Station, Pa. 17728

SOUTH CAROLINA

South Carolina Chapter, P.O. Box 12112, Columbia, S.C. 29211

SOUTH DAKOTA

Dacotah Chapter, P.O. Box 1624, Rapid City, S.D. 57701

TENNESSEE

Tennessee Chapter, c/o Kelly, 107 Vista Dr., Chattanooga, Tenn. 37411

TEXAS

Lone Star Chapter, P.O. Box 1931, Austin, Tex. 78767.

UTAH

Utah Chapter, Utah Environmental Center, P.O. Box 8393, Salt Lake City, Utah 84108

VIRGINIA

Old Dominion Chapter, c/o Fulghum, 13412 Woodbriar Ridge, Midlothian, Va. 23113

WASHINGTON

Cascade Chapter, 4534½ University Way NE, Seattle, Wash. 98105
Northern Rockies Chapter, c/o Bond, P.O. Box 424, Spokane, Wash. 99210

WISCONSIN

John Muir Chapter, 444 W. Main Street, Madison, Wis. 53703

WYOMING

Wyoming Chapter, P.O. Box 1595, Cody, Wyo. 82414

CANADA

Western Canada Chapter, Box 35520, Station E, Vancouver, British Columbia, Canada V6M 4G8
Ontario Chapter, 47 Colbourne St., Suite 308, Toronto, Ontario, Canada M5M 1E3

## The Appalachian Trail Conference

The ATC is a consortium of 60 East Coast hiking and skiing clubs that support and maintain the 2,000 mile Appalachian Trail, running from Springer Mountain in northern Georgia to Mt. Katahdin in northern Maine. Information about the overall trail can be obtained by writing to the ATC itself. If you are more interested in local hiking or backpacking, write to one of the following 22 more active ATC member clubs.

The Appalachian Trail Conference, Inc.
P.O. Box 236
Harpers Ferry, W. Va. 25425
(304) 535-6331
* * * * * * * *

## GEORGIA

Georgia Appalachian Trail Club
Ms. Margaret Drummond, President
1351 Springdale Rd.
Atlanta, Ga. 30306

## MAINE

Maine Appalachian Trail Club
Dave Field, President
Box 183-A, RFD #2
Bangor, Me. 04401

## MARYLAND

Mountain Club of Maryland
Paul Ives, President
802 Kingston Rd.
Baltimore, Md. 21212

## NEW YORK

New York/New Jersey Trail Conference
Albert Field, Executive Director
15 E. 40th St.
New York, N.Y. 10016

## NORTH CAROLINA
Carolina Mountain Club
John Tompkins, President
1 Baird Mountain Rd.
Asheville, N.C. 28804

Nantahala Hiking Club
Donald W. McLean, President
Rt. 1, Box 162
Franklin, N.C. 28734

Piedmont Appalachian Trail Hikers
Tom Harman, President
307 S. Chapman
Greensboro, N.C. 27403

## PENNSYLVANIA

Allentown Hiking Club
Bill Bevan, President
124 S. 16th St.
Allentown, Penn. 18102

Keystone Trails Association
Maurice J. Forrester, Jr., President
Road 3, Box 261, Factory Rd.
Cogan Station, Penn. 17728

Blue Mountain Eagle Climbers Club
Leonard L. Reed, Sr., President
122 W. High St.
Wormlesdorf, Penn. 19567

Susquehanna Appalachian Trail Club
Mary W. Ludes, President
87 Greenwood Circle
Wormlesburg, Penn. 17043

RHODE ISLAND

Appalachian Mountain Club, Narragansett Chapter
Earl Perkins, President
130-A Willard Ave.
Wakefield, R.I. 02879

TENNESSEE

Tennessee Eastman Hiking Club
Robert W. Miller, President
P.O. Box 511, Bldg. 215
Kingsport, Tenn. 37662

Smoky Mountain Hiking Club
Sam Tillet, President
P.O. Box 1454
Knoxville, Tenn. 37901

VERMONT

The Green Mountain Club
Joseph E. Frank, President
31 Bilodeau Parkway
Burlington, Vt. 05401

VIRGINIA

Mt. Rogers Appalachian Trail Club
Dan Schunke, President
29 Shadow Grove Circle
Bristol, Va. 24201

Natural Bridge Appalachian Trail Club
G.A. McDaniel, III, President
P.O. Box 3156
Lynchburg, Va. 24503

Old Dominion Appalachian Trail Club
P.O. Box 25283
Richmond, Va. 23260

Roanoke Appalachian Trail Club
John W. Bowles, President
2416 Stanley Ave. SE
Roanoke, Va. 24014

Tidewater Appalachian Trail Club
Mike Ashe, President
P.O. Box 62044
Virginia Beach, Va. 23462

WASHINGTON, D.C.

Potomac Appalachian Trail Club
Scott Johnson, President
1718 "N" St., NW
Washington, D.C. 20036

WEST VIRGINIA

Kanawha Trail Club
Vito C. Hughes, President
P.O. Box 2652
Charleston, W. Va. 25330

**Other organizations of interest**

Friends of the Earth
124 Spear St.
San Francisco, Calif. 94105

Mazamas
909 NW 19th Ave.
Portland, Ore. 97209

The Mountaineers
719 Pike St.
Seattle, Wash. 98101

National Audubon Society
950 Third Ave.
New York, N.Y. 10022

Pacific Crest Trail Conference
Hotel Green
50 Green St.
Pasadena, Calif.

The Wilderness Society
1901 Pennsylvania Ave. NW
Washington, D.C. 20006

## Jogging and other sports

For information on the awards programs for jogging, running, and back-packing mentioned in chapter 1, write to the following:

National Jogging Association
919 18th St., NW, Suite 803
Washington, D.C. 20006

Presidential Sports Awards
Greene, R.I. 02827

## Commercial Tour Organizors

Best Tours
3010 Santa Monica Blvd., #307
Santa Monica, Calif. 90404
(213) 390-6858

Canyon Explorers Club
1223 Frances Ave.
Fullerton, Calif. 92631
(714) 879-3741

EarthTrek Expeditions & Travel
1540 E. Edinger
Santa Ana, Calif.
(714) 547-5864

High Country Adventures
P.O. Box 176
Helena, Mont. 59601
(406) 443-2842

Mountain Travel, Inc.
1398 Solana Ave.
Albany, Calif. 94706
(415) 527-8100

Nature Expeditions International
599 College Ave.
Palo Alto, Calif. 94306
(415) 328-6572

Sierra Club Outing Department
The Sierra Club
530 Bush St.
San Francisco, Calif. 94108

Wilderness Expeditions
P.O. Box 5041
Riverside, Calif. 92517
(714) 684-1227

# About the Author

W.R.C. Shedenhelm is the 55-year-old senior editor of the nationally distributed rockhounding and lapidary monthly magazine, *ROCK & GEM,* published in Encino, California. For recreation he backpacks alone and with his 13-year-old son, Richard. He has earned six Presidential Sports Awards, four of them for backpacking. He is a former chairman of the Backpacking Committee of the 23,000-member Angeles Chapter of the Sierra Club, and has led backpacking and climbing trips in California's Sierra Nevada and on the Mexican volcanos.

In addition to hundreds of magazine articles in the fields of automotives, backpacking, rockhounding, and humor, Shedenhelm has authored and photo-illustrated books on backpacking (Fawcett 1972, Petersen 1974), motor-cycles and trail bikes (Pyramid-Jove 1973, 1974, 1976, 1977), and "The Young Rockhound's Handbook" (G.P. Putnam's Sons 1978).

A graduate of Columbia University, he is a member of the Academy of Magical Arts, the Astronomical League, the American Association for the Advancement of Science, the Geological Society of America, the Sierra Club, and the Ancient and Honorable Order of E Clampus Vitus.

# Recommended Reading

**Rocky Mountain National Park Trail Guide** by Erik Nilsson

*Rocky Mountain National Park Trail Guide* is an informative guide to the trails and scenic features of the park. The book features topographical maps of the park and practical information. Paperback, $3.95.

**Skin Care for Men and Women Outdoors** by Cameron Smith, M.D.

*Skin Care for Men and Women Outdoors* is an active person's medical bible. As every outdoor person knows, nature can be rough on the skin. Injuries to the skin come from all sides—from the sun, wind, and rain, from plants, animals, and bugs, from the fire we cook with, the food we eat, even the clothes we wear. Hardback, $10.00.

**Guide to Inflatable Canoes and Kayaks** by William Sanders

With the current influx of inflatable canoes and kayaks into the market-place, the *Guide to Inflatable Canoes and Kayaks* is just the consumer aid river enthusiasts have been searching for. Sanders, an experienced river runner and outdoorsman, explores every important aspect of running the rapids skillfully and safely. Paperback, $5.95.

**River Rafting** by Cecil Kuhne

*River Rafting* provides a comprehensive discussion of rowing and paddling strokes, turns, techniques for handling the raft through a variety of water levels and weather conditions, and raft rescue. Wilderness camping is explored in detail, as is raft selection, maintenance, and repair. Paperback, $4.95.

**Runner's Cookbook** by Joanne Milkereit with Hal Higdon

Every running household will want a copy of the *Runner's Cookbook* in the kitchen. Anyone who runs and enjoys a good meal will find it chock full of recipes and anecdotes to delight the stomach and the mind. And anyone who runs competitively will appreciate the nutritional and pre-race information. Spiral bound, $14.95.

Available in fine bookstores and sport shops, or from:

## World Publications, Inc.

Box 366, Mountain View, CA 94042

**Include $.45 shipping and handling for each title (Maximum $2.25).**

## DATE DUE